BIBLE QUIZZES FOR EVERYBODY

BIBLE QUIZZES FOR EVERYBODY

By
Frederick Hall

BAKER BOOK HOUSE
Grand Rapids, Michigan

ISBN: 0-8010-4032-9

Copyright, 1941, by
Baker Book House Company

Third printing, November 1973

Printed in the United States of America

TO THE MEMORY OF MY MOTHER:
Because of whom Bible Quizzes, for me,
have always been easy.

TABLE OF CONTENTS

Section I
QUIZZES FOR CHILDREN
Quizzes	9
Answers	20

Section II
THINGS THAT JESUS SAID
Quizzes	27
Answers	37

Section III
WHO SAID IT?
Quizzes	42
Answers	46

Section IV
BIBLE ACQUAINTANCES
Quizzes	50
Answers	61

Section V
BOOKS OF THE BIBLE
Quizzes	62
Answers	75

Section VI

BIBLE TRIPLETS

Quizzes 76
Answers 97

Section VII

THE BIBLE AND THE POETS

Quizzes 101
Answers 115

Section VIII

MISCELLANEOUS QUIZZES

Quizzes 120
Answers 137

FOREWORD

Most of these Bible Quizzes have appeared, during the past three or four years, in various religious and secular publications and are here reprinted partly because editors have had requests for them in book form.

In quoting the Bible, the King James version is commonly used as being more familiar, though other translations, the American Standard and Prof. Edgar Goodspeed's American Translation of the New Testament, are sometimes employed. In a few instances, the writer has ventured to paraphrase.

While some of the quizzes are for children, they are not "graded," save that in a general way the more difficult are toward the end.

When, as occasionally happens, the same character appears under different headings, it is not to be assumed that this is due to oversight. Met a second time, a "Bible Acquaintance" will, it is hoped, be the more easily recognized. Similarly, the same Bible story is sometimes presented both in outline and more fully, or from a child's and later from an adult's point of view.

Recognized authorities, notably Hastings' *Dictionary of the Bible,* are occasionally quoted but the writer, a layman, has not sought to interpret, or to present any individual or controversial point of view, as might easily have been done—even in a book of Bible quizzes.

By way of personal confession: the writer came to know the Bible where it can be best learned, at a mother's knee, since there one learns to both know and love it. During the years of adolescence and maturity he has read it, he hopes, with increasing understanding. From a full heart he can echo the words of one of the great teachers of our time: ". . . the Bible from the start was an integral part of myself, and it would be as absurd to attempt an estimate of what I owe to it as it would be to appraise what I owe to my lungs or to my heart." To make it a source of mere diversion (however wholesome) prompts to apology: and yet, perhaps, through even this humble channel, some one may be brought back to its pages there to find renewal of interest.

The Bible, as has been often said, is so much more than a book—it is a literature. To become saturated with this literature is to have one's whole life immeasurably enriched and fortified.

FREDERICK HALL.

Berea, Kentucky.

BIBLE QUIZZES FOR EVERYBODY

Section I
QUIZZES FOR CHILDREN

No. 1. THE BIBLE
Some Questions About It

1. Every year the leading book stores of our country list what they call the "best sellers" but every year one book always outsells the best of the best sellers. What is it?
2. Was the Bible, or any part of it, first written in English?
3. Is the Bible one book or is it really a number of books bound together?
4. The Bible contains many of the words of Jesus but did he write any of them himself?

No. 2. BIBLE GEOGRAPHY
What Can You Tell About the Holy Land?

1. In the northern part of the country in which Jesus lived, the Holy Land, as we sometimes call it, was a beautiful little lake. Jesus often crossed it, more than once he preached upon its shores, some of his friends earned their living by fishing in it. What was its name?
2. Out of this lake the River Jordan—the only large river of the country—flows south into a sort of great sink hole, that has no outlet. It is below sea level and it is so salty that no fish can live in it. Also, no swimmer can sink in it. What is its name?

[Answers on pages 20–21]

3. Surrounded by mountains was a city which Jesus loved. Into its temple he had been taken as a baby. He returned to it as a boy. He taught there as a man and entered its gates in triumph. Outside its walls he met his death. What is the name of the city?

4. The Phœnicians, living north of the Holy Land, were at one time great sailors. The Jews did not like sailing; nevertheless their whole western boundary was a body of water which they called the Great Sea. What do we call it?

No. 3. BIBLE PICTURES

If some day you were showing a book of Bible pictures to a child too small to read, what would you tell him about pictures like these?

1. A great expanse of water—no land in sight anywhere. One huge boat, without sails, and, from a window in the boat, a man's hand reaching out for a bird having a leaf in its beak.

2. A great tower, still unfinished, but so high that its top is hidden by clouds.

3. A fight between a man and a lion. The man has no gun, sword or spear, just his bare hands, and yet the lion is getting the worst of it.

4. A terrible looking man, dressed in armor, and carrying sword and spear. Running toward him a boy armed with nothing but a sling.

5. A man seated at the center of a long table, with twelve other men, six on either side of him.

No. 4. THE BOY JESUS

1. In what town was Jesus born?
2. In what town did he grow up? (Strange as it may seem, it was a town with a bad reputation.)
3. Was Jesus the only child in the home, or were there others?
4. We are told but one story of Jesus' boyhood. What was it?
5. Excepting for this story, almost all that we know of Jesus as a boy is found in three verses of the second chapter of Luke. Can you tell, in your own words, any of the things they say?

[Answers on pages 20–21]

No. 5. THE MAN JESUS

1. Did Jesus begin to teach and preach as soon as he became a man?
2. When Jesus began his teaching, a group of friends joined him, partly to be taught by him, partly to help him in his work. What do we usually call them?
3. One time, when Jesus' friends had heard him praying, they asked him to teach them to pray. He did, warning them first not to use "vain repetitions." What was the model prayer he gave them?
4. After Jesus had gone from the earth, his life was written by four different men who loved him and these lives are the first four books in our New Testament. By what names are they called?

No. 6. PICTURES OF JESUS

1. Some pictures show Jesus' mother holding him and sitting upon a donkey which Joseph is leading. Can you tell where they are going?
2. You have probably seen pictures of Jesus and his mother with an older boy. Do you know who this older boy was?
3. Many pictures of the boy Jesus show him among shavings by a work bench. Why should he not be shown watching sheep or planting a garden?
4. A famous picture shows the boy Jesus standing among a group of bearded men. What can you tell about this picture?

No. 7. THINGS JESUS SAID

1. What did Jesus say about the wild flowers—the lilies of the field?
2. What did he say about the birds—the fowls of the air?
3. What did he say about the sparrows?
4. Jesus said the peacemakers should be called—What?
5. Jesus said, "Blessed are the pure in heart," and then gave what reason for it?

[Answers on pages 21–22]

No. 8. THINGS PAUL DID

1. Before Paul became a follower of Jesus, he once watched a bad thing done. He did not help in it—or try to prevent it. All his after life he was sorry. What was it?
2. Besides teaching and preaching, Paul had a trade at which he sometimes worked to earn his living. What was it?
3. Paul wanted to go to Rome. At last his chance came and he went. As a tourist? As a travelling workman? As a sailor? As a stowaway? How?
4. During the voyage to Rome such a terrible storm arose that for many days they could see neither the sun nor the stars. Was the ship wrecked or saved?
5. Paul had a young friend whom he loved greatly and to whom he wrote two letters, found in our New Testament. What was the young man's name?

No. 9. THE JOURNEY OF ABRAHAM'S SERVANT

In Bible times marriages were arranged by parents and, when Abraham's son Isaac was old enough to marry, his father wanted for him a wife from among their own people. But this could not be easily arranged, for Abraham was a pioneer living far from all his relatives.

Finally he called to him his most trusted servant and sent him on the long journey to the land from which, many years before, Abraham had come. There he was to find Isaac a wife. Many days he travelled. He realized how important his mission was and, as one should do when faced with heavy responsibility, he prayed about it. Then one evening the caravan neared the journey's end and, coming down to the well, with a pitcher upon her shoulder, he saw ——

What happened next?

No. 10. THE RUNAWAY

He did not run away because he wanted to but because he was afraid to stay at home and, worse still, he ought to have been afraid. He had taken advantage of his careless, reckless brother

[Answers on pages 22–23]

and had cheated him. He had fooled his father, who had always been kind to him. He had been mean, and tricky, and underhanded: and such a boy is of course headed straight for trouble. He was hurrying and he was all alone, when one night—perhaps his first night—he made camp in a desolate and desert place. The people of that time understood less about God than we do today and he probably imagined that in leaving home he was leaving not only his father and mother but God too. And then ——
What happened next?

No. 11. BOYHOOD OF A PRIME MINISTER

He must have been a singularly attractive boy but he was not born wise (no boy is) and some things that he did led him into sore trouble. He was his father's "pet" which is not altogether surprising, for his older brothers were a rough lot. His father showed him special favors (gave him better clothes for one thing) and perhaps he took advantage of this favoritism. From the beginning, he seems to have been certain that some day he would be a great man, greater than his brothers or even his father. There may not have been so much harm in that but he talked about it, which of course was neither modest nor sensible. It made his brothers angry but that was no excuse for their doing the wicked thing they did, which was ——
What happened next?

No. 12. THE BABY WHO WAS HIDDEN

Long ago a Hebrew baby was born into a world so dangerous that a cruel law forbade his even living in it. Naturally, however, his mother paid no attention to that law: she kept him hidden. Then, when he was three months old and perhaps because the house was no longer a safe place for him, she made him a little boat (an ark the Bible calls it) and laid it among the rushes in the shallow water of the river, while not far off his sister watched closely. All at once, she saw some people coming and ——
What happened next?

[Answers on page 23]

No. 13. HOW THE TREES CHOSE A KING

This is not as familiar as most of the stories we have been reading. It is a fable, a Bible not an Æsop fable, and it was first told at the risk of a man's life, to make fun of another man who had made himself king.

Once upon a time, he said, the trees decided to form a kingdom and going to the olive tree asked if he would reign over them. But the olive tree said it was out of the question: he must attend to his olives, which seemed to him far more important. He would not be their king.

Next they tried the fig tree but he reminded them of the figs that he must bear. They would have to find some one else. *He* could not be their king.

The grape vine said much the same thing and so, finally, they went to the useless bramble, which bore no fruit at all and ——

What happened next?

No. 14. THE VOICE IN THE NIGHT

Like other boys, he had a father and mother, who loved him as he loved them, but he did not live with them. For as long as he could remember, he had lived in the temple and slept near Eli, the High Priest, who had been to him like a kindly grandfather. Now Eli was old and growing blind and the boy spent much of his time waiting on him.

On this night, the boy lay down as usual. "The lamp was burning dim before the sacred ark." He did not go to sleep at once and, suddenly, he thought he heard some one call his name. He ran to Eli but the old priest said, "No. I did not call you. Lie down again." A second and then a third time, he thought he heard the voice and then ——

What happened next?

No. 15. THE SHEEP TENDER

It sounds almost like a fairy tale.

Once upon a time, there lived a boy whose business it was to go out into the fields each day and look after his father's sheep.

14   [Answers on pages 23–24]

(His older brothers—he had a half dozen or more of them—did the heavier and more important work.) Tending sheep could sometimes be dangerous. Once he had to fight a lion and another time a bear. But usually it was easy and gave him much time in which he might have been idle—but wasn't: instead he practiced hour after hour with his sling, until he learned to throw very far and straight. Sometimes too he practiced on his harp—a very different sort of harp from any you may have seen.

Then one day, when he was alone in the field, some one came running and called to him that a great man was at their house and wanted to see *him*.

What happened next?

No. 16. THE LITTLE SLAVE GIRL

In a long ago, cruel time, a little girl whose name is not told us was carried off to be a slave in a far-away land. At first she must have been very unhappy. Later it was better, for she seems to have been kindly treated. Her mistress was the wife of a man who in our time would be called a general. Every one respected him and every one was sorry for him, because he had a terrible disease called leprosy, which at that time no doctor knew how to cure. The little girl, however, felt sure that a man named Elisha, who lived in her own country, could, with God's help, make him well again. She told her mistress about it and, when her mistress told the general, he seemed to think it worth trying, for messengers and presents were sent to the king of the little girl's country, asking him to arrange to have the general cured. Then ——

What happened next?

No. 17. THE BOY KING

His name was Jehoash—sometimes spelled Joash. When he was a baby, his brothers and cousins were all killed, through the influence of a wicked woman who wished to make herself queen —and did. She would have killed him too, had she known about him, but an aunt hid him, first in the lumber room of the palace and then in the temple, where he lived month after month, year

[Answers on page 24]

after year, guarded by the chief priest, Jehoida, and a few brave and faithful friends, who kept his secret. He probably never went outside the temple enclosure and never knew that he was the rightful heir to a throne.

Then, one day, when he was seven years old ——

What happened next?

No. 18. A BIRTHDAY STORY

This story is about some men who were frightened and later made glad. You have heard it many times. It happened near a famous little village not far from Jerusalem, in which once a king had been born. As a boy, never dreaming of the greatness that was to come to him, he had tended sheep on these very hills where tonight men were tending sheep, men who never guessed that this was to be the most wonderful night of all the years.

We can imagine them, "all seated on the ground," and how startled they were when "the angel of the Lord appeared and glory shone around." Spellbound they listened until, faintly, the angel chorus of peace on earth, good will to men died away and then ——

What happened next?

No. 19. LEAVING BETHLEHEM

You have seen many pictures of them: the men led by the star, coming riding upon their camels into Bethlehem, there opening their gifts, gold, frankincense and myrrh, and kneeling at the manger side to offer them to the baby Jesus. It is said they were kings. One of our Christmas hymns calls them Three Kings of Orient. There are books in which their names are given but most of this is uncertainty. The Bible gives us no names. It does not tell us their rank or how many of them there were. It calls them Wise Men from the East and says that, when they came and saw the young child with Mary his mother, they fell down and worshipped him. After they were gone ——

What happened next?

[Answers on page 24]

No. 20. THE BOY WHO WAS LOST

The greatest holiday of the Jewish people was their Passover, in which was something of our Thanksgiving, something of our Independence Day (July 4th). Every year as many people as could went to celebrate it in Jerusalem, their capital city. Mary and Joseph went whenever possible and the year Jesus was twelve years old, they took him along.

It was more than a single day's journey. At night they "camped out." It must have been great fun. The wonderful celebration in the city! The sight-seeing! The journey home again! This time no one happened to see the boy Jesus when they started back but all were sure he was there somewhere and then ——

What happened next?

No. 21. THE BOY WITH THE LUNCH

In the days when Jesus was teaching, preaching and healing, many people followed him eagerly for long distances, so anxious to see and hear him that sometimes they forgot how far from home it was, forgot even to eat and at last found themselves tired and very hungry.

Once, when Jesus saw a great company of such people, he was sorry for them and asked one of his disciples where to buy them food. The disciple, I imagine, must have been puzzled. Food for such a crowd ——! In our money it would have taken forty dollars. They were poor men. Had they that much? It is doubtful and, even if they had, certainly no store or bakery was near.

"There is a boy though," one disciple said, "who has five barley loaves and a couple of fish."

"Make the people sit down," said Jesus.

They sat down and then ——

What happened next?

No. 22. A FISHING STORY

Often, when Jesus was preaching and teaching, crowds fol-

[Answers on pages 24–25]

lowed him and we read of how one time, when he was upon the lake shore, they pressed so close that only those nearest could hear well and some were in danger of getting wet. So Jesus asked if he might borrow a fishing boat and the owner, whose name was Peter, said he might. The boat was anchored a little way off shore. Jesus sat down in it and talked and in this way more people could see and hear him.

Afterward, wanting perhaps to repay Peter for his loan of the boat, Jesus told him to go out into the lake and try again to catch some fish. Peter said they had been fishing all night and had not caught a thing but he would do whatever Jesus suggested.

Then he and his brother Andrew went out, lowered their net and ——

What happened next?

No. 23. A ROBBER STORY

A certain man, Jesus once told his friends, was travelling a dangerous road they all knew well and was set upon by robbers. They must have been very wicked and cruel men, for not only did they take everything he had—even his clothes, but they beat him so badly that, when they went away, he lay helpless beside the road, bleeding and half dead. Then, one by one, along that road, came three other men. The business of the first was to help people but he did nothing: he passed by on the other side. The second did not help either—he may have been afraid. Then the third man, a foreigner, came and ——

What happened next?

No. 24. THE LOST SHEEP

From the very beginning, the Jewish people had kept sheep and a thousand times Jesus' disciples must have seen shepherds with their flocks. They probably knew the twenty-third Psalm too, "The Lord is my Shepherd," as well as we do. So it was quite natural that, when Jesus wanted to tell them a story, to teach them something, he would make his story about a shepherd.

Take one of them, he said, who had a hundred sheep. He may

[Answers on pages 25–26]

have known every one of them by name. (Some shepherds did.) At any rate he knew exactly how *many* he had and, when he found that one was missing ——

What happened next?

No. 25. THE BUSINESS MAN

When Jesus told this story, he did not tell what sort of business the man was in but, at any rate, he had a number of other men working for him and he had to take a trip into " a far country." He of course did not want his business to stop while he was away and so he decided to leave some money with his men and see how well each could do on " his own." He called them one by one and, because he must already have had a pretty good idea of their ability, he did not give them all the same amount but to one five thousand dollars, to another two thousand, another one and so on. Your Bible will say he gave them " talents." Putting the money into thousands of dollars (Goodspeed's translation) gives you some idea of how much a talent is.

He went away then but, after a long time, he came back and ——

What happened next?

[Answers on page 26]

ANSWERS

Section I
QUIZZES FOR CHILDREN

No. 1. THE BIBLE

1. The Bible.
2. No, it was first written in Hebrew and Greek, in days before printing was invented and before there was any such language as English. Hundreds of years later, it was translated into all modern languages so that any one might be able to read it in his own tongue.
3. A number of books: indeed it is almost a library. Books of history, biography, prophecy, poetry, legal books, one hymn book, one play (drama) and several other kinds of writing all combine to make up our Bible.
4. No. The New Testament tells us of but one time when Jesus wrote. Then he stooped down and wrote with his finger on the ground—and *what* he wrote we do not know.

No. 2. BIBLE GEOGRAPHY

1. The Sea of Galilee.
2. The Dead Sea.
3. Jerusalem.
4. The Mediterranean Sea.

No. 3. BIBLE PICTURES

You would probably tell the child:
1. That is Noah, reaching his hand out of the ark to take in the dove that he had sent to see if the waters of the flood had gone down (Gen. 8).

2. The Tower of Babel, which men started to build with the foolish idea of climbing up into heaven (Gen. 11).

3. Samson, about whose great strength the Bible tells such wonderful stories (Judges 14: 5–6).

4. David going out to fight the giant Goliath (I Sam. 17).

5. The Last Supper eaten by Jesus with his disciples, the one we celebrate in our communion.

No. 4. THE BOY JESUS

1. In Bethlehem of Judea.

2. In Nazareth of Galilee (John 1: 46).

3. There were others—he was the oldest (Matt. 13: 55–56).

4. The story of the time when he went up to Jerusalem, with Joseph and Mary, for the Feast of the Passover and was found by them in the temple, " in the midst of the doctors, both hearing them and asking them questions " (Luke 2: 41–50).

5. The verses tell us (Goodspeed's translation) that he " became strong and thoughtful, with God's blessing resting on him," that he was obedient to his parents and that, as he grew older, " he gained in wisdom and won the approval of God and men " (Luke 2: 40, 51, 52).

No. 5. THE MAN JESUS

1. No; he waited until he was thirty. Joseph, it is believed, had died. Jesus was the oldest son and for ten years he (probably) worked as a carpenter to support his mother and younger brothers and sisters.

2. We usually call them the twelve apostles—or disciples.

3. The Lord's Prayer. Can you repeat it?

4. Matthew. Mark. Luke. John.

No. 6. PICTURES OF JESUS

1. They are going into Egypt, to escape from a wicked king who wanted to kill Jesus.

2. His name was John; later he came to be known as John the Baptist. (His mother and Jesus' mother were related.)

3. Joseph was a carpenter and his shop was of course the place where Jesus would play and later work.

4. Jesus was in the temple, listening to the teachers there and asking them questions. He was surprised that any one looking for him should not have looked there first.

No. 7. THINGS JESUS SAID

1. That they did not work, neither toil nor spin, and yet are dressed more beautifully than was King Solomon in all his glory (Matt. 6: 28–29).

2. That they sow no seed, harvest no crops, put nothing away for the winter and yet God feeds them (Matt. 6: 26).

3. That they are almost worthless (two of them sold for a farthing—a cent) yet God watches over them (Matt. 10: 29).

4. The children of God (Matt. 5: 9).

5. ". . . for they shall see God" (Matt. 5: 8).

No. 8. THINGS PAUL DID

1. The stoning of Stephen (Acts 7: 58–Acts 8: 1).

2. Making tents (Acts 18: 3).

3. As a prisoner (Acts 27: 1).

4. The ship was wrecked but the people on it were all saved (Acts 27 and 28).

5. Timothy.

No. 9. THE JOURNEY OF ABRAHAM'S SERVANT

You have probably guessed it: a young woman—the very one he would have chosen. She and her people received him kindly. The next day she started back with him and the Bible tells us how they made the return journey safely and she became Isaac's wife and he loved her. (You will find the whole story in the twenty-fourth chapter of Genesis.)

No. 10. THE RUNAWAY

A wonderful dream came to him, a dream we still sing about

in the negro spiritual, *Jacob's Ladder.* It taught him that he was not leaving God—God could go with him. And right there he made up his mind to do better and promised God that he would. (You will find the whole story in Genesis 28: 11-22.)

No. 11. BOYHOOD OF A PRIME MINISTER

They sold him as a slave and made their father believe that a wild animal had killed him. The boy, whose name was Joseph, was carried into Egypt where, after slavery and imprisonment, he rose to be the second most important person in the kingdom. (You will find the whole story in the thirty-seventh chapter of Genesis and those that follow.)

No. 12. THE BABY WHO WAS HIDDEN

The approaching people were a princess and her ladies-in-waiting. They saw the baby, one of them brought it to her mistress and, when it cried, the princess was sorry for it and decided to adopt it. She would need a nurse, the sister reminded her, and when the princess said yes, the clever sister brought the baby's own mother. The baby grew up to be the great law-giver of his nation. (You will find the whole story in the second chapter of Exodus.)

No. 13. HOW THE TREES CHOSE A KING

The bramble said, "Certainly. I will be your king and a very great king." But one suspects that he was mistaken. (You will find the whole story in Judges 9: 7-15.)

No. 14. THE VOICE IN THE NIGHT

Eli told him what to answer and to the boy, whose name was Samuel, was given a sad message. He felt almost afraid to deliver it and yet in the morning, when Eli asked him about it, he told everything. (You will find the whole story in I Samuel 3.)

No. 15. THE SHEEP TENDER

He found that the great man was Samuel the Prophet and that he was come to say that the boy (whose name was David) would some day be king of all his people. (You will find the whole story in I Samuel 16.)

No. 16. THE LITTLE SLAVE GIRL

The king thought they were trying to pick a quarrel with him, but, when Elisha heard of it, he sent for the general and finally he was cured. (You will find the whole story in II Kings 5.)

No. 17. THE BOY KING

Led by Jehoida, the palace bodyguard revolted, the wicked queen was overthrown and Jehoash was made king. Guided by the counsels of the wise old priest, he brought better times for every one. (You will find the whole story in II Kings 11.)

No. 18. A BIRTHDAY STORY

The shepherds said one to another, " Let us now go even unto Bethlehem, and see this thing which is come to pass, which the Lord hath made known unto us." (You will find the whole story in the second chapter of Luke—or perhaps you know it well enough to repeat it.)

No. 19. LEAVING BETHLEHEM

A dream made Joseph realize that to stay longer in Judea would be dangerous. So he took the baby Jesus and his mother and fled into Egypt, where they stayed until they could return safely. (You will find the whole story in the second chapter of Matthew, verses 12–15.)

No. 20. THE BOY WHO WAS LOST

After a day's journey, finding him nowhere in the company, Joseph and Mary anxiously hurried back to Jerusalem. There, after three days, they found him in the temple, among the learned teachers of the law and, the Bible tells us, "all that heard him were astonished at his understanding and answers" (Luke 2:47). Had he perhaps become so interested that he forgot all about going home? (You will find the whole story in the second chapter of Luke.)

No. 21. THE BOY WITH THE LUNCH

In some way that we do not understand, they all had enough to eat and food was left over. (You will find the whole story in John 6.)

No. 22. A FISHING STORY

The net enclosed so many fish that they had to call their partners, James and John, who came with another boat to help them. Peter had been fishing for years but never had he seen anything like this and it frightened him, as you might be frightened by something for which you had no explanation. Jesus smiled at him (I *think* he smiled, though the Bible does not say so) and told him not to be afraid: from now on he would catch men.

What do you suppose Jesus meant by that?

(You will find the whole story in Luke 5:1–10.)

No. 23. A ROBBER STORY

He gave the man first aid, put him upon his own animal and took him to a place where he could be cared for and could rest up. Next morning, when leaving, he paid the man's bill and told the innkeeper that he would be good for any more that he might have to spend on him. (You will find the whole story in the tenth chapter of Luke.)

No. 24. THE LOST SHEEP

He did not say, "Well, that's too bad but it's the sheep's own fault and, anyhow, I have ninety-nine others. Maybe tomorrow it will come back." He left the ninety-and-nine (in a safe place, we may be sure) and went hunting the lost one until he found it. God, Jesus said, is like that. When some one wanders away from him and gets into trouble, he does not wait for him to come back. He goes after him and, when he finds him, "joy shall be in heaven." (You will find the whole story in Luke 15: 4–7).

No. 25. THE BUSINESS MAN

He received reports from the men who worked for him. All had done well and were praised and rewarded, excepting the one to whom had been given the one thousand dollars. All he had done with it was to bury it in the ground and then dig it up again, when he heard that his master had come home.

Jesus said we are somewhat like those men. God has put us here, he has given us abilities—" talents "—and he expects us to make the very best use of them.

(You will find the whole story in Matthew 25: 14–30.)

Section II
THINGS THAT JESUS SAID

Even in our own time, there have been powerful rulers who have not liked the Bible and its teachings. Suppose (there is no likelihood that it will ever happen but just *suppose*) that such a dictator were to make a law that three fourths of the contents of the Bible must be destroyed. Which parts would every lover of the Bible agree must be kept?

There would of course be some difference of opinion but practically all would say that the words spoken by Jesus are the most precious ever recorded.

The quizzes of this group may all be answered in his words.

No. 1

The greatest sermon ever preached was of course the Sermon on the Mount, found in the 5th, 6th and 7th chapters of Matthew's gospel. One reason for its greatness is that it treats of such common—and important—things; things every one of us must think about, if we would lead useful and happy lives. Some of them are suggested in the following questions. How many can you answer?

1. Pretty clothes! Who would imagine finding in this sermon anything about that subject? But it is there. First decide what you yourself think of their importance. Then try to remember whether Jesus ever said anything about them. (You need not quote his exact words.)

2. In a sermon as inclusive as this, one would expect to find something about war. But (at least by that name) it is not mentioned. Jesus does not say, in so many words, "You must not fight." What he does do is to give a command far more radical and harder to obey. What is it?

3. Jesus' countrymen, you will remember, lived under the rule

[Answers on page 37]

of the Romans—and did not like it. Suppose you had been one of them and a Roman soldier had ordered you to go a mile with him, perhaps to show him the road, perhaps to carry part of his equipment. What ought you to do?

4. All of us are sadly apt, at times, to go looking for other people's faults, instead of seeing the good and pleasant things about them. (Worse still, we sometimes enjoy telling a " bad " thing some friend or acquaintance has done.) What does Jesus say about this?

5. Philosophers and religious teachers, who have tried to bring men to lead the good life, have never told us that it was easy. They are pretty well agreed however that it is simple—a few rules will cover it. What is Jesus' condensed rule for right living?

No. 2

Years ago a trustee of a well-known American college offered five dollars to every student who would commit to memory the Sermon on the Mount. I knew one girl who learned the three chapters from Matthew in which it is found and, entirely apart from the money, it was, I think, well worth her while. However, it is of course far more important to know and to apply the principles of these wonderful verses than it is to be able to repeat them word for word. Bear that in mind, as you try to answer the following questions.

1. Savages are always dogged by fears and one especially: that their gods are hostile and on the watch to " get " them. Jesus taught that this pagan feeling, sometimes found even among Christians, is all wrong. Earthly parents, imperfect as they are, yet love to give good things to their children; from this we may naturally and properly infer—What?

2. " Thou shalt not kill . . . Thou shalt not steal . . . Honor thy father and thy mother." All these commandments and the other seven, a young man once told Jesus, he had kept from his youth up. But there are other sins besides those mentioned in the decalog: the sin of worry, for instance, which, if persisted in, may become a dangerous disease. Can you think of any warning that Jesus ever gave against it?

3. In one part of this sermon, Jesus speaks of a fig tree and a grape vine, using them as illustrations of the fact that it is not

[Answers on page 37]

hard to tell who is a really good person. The rule, as simple and sensible as any one could ask, is—What?

4. Years hence our century will be known as one of road building. Jesus too lived in a road-building time and, in this sermon, he talks about two roads, one broad and easy to travel, the other narrow and difficult. Which one did he advise his friends to take—and why?

5. Have you ever stopped to think how very few people—often not more than one or two—will set the standard for a whole community and make it really worth while? Jesus expected his followers to do that and, to illustrate it, he compared them with something that all of us eat every day of our lives. What is it?

No. 3

Children in Sunday Schools once had to commit to memory many verses. (I myself once heard a girl stand up and recite over one thousand—rapidly and with very little idea of their meaning.) Today we know that to understand a verse is better than to be able to repeat it, though to be able to repeat it is also a good thing. The following questions can be answered by things Jesus said but his exact words need not be given.

1. Ask a hundred persons, "What is the best thing that could come to the world today?" and many of them would answer, "A just and lasting peace." But Jesus knew that peace does not just "come"; it must be "made." What did he say about the peace makers?

2. The friends of Jesus lived happy lives but not because they had no troubles—they were happy in spite of their troubles. Jesus never said, "You are fortunate when every one treats you well and says nice things about you." Instead he said something startlingly different. What was it?

3. Can you imagine a good person living day after day among other people and no neighbor ever finding out that he was good? Such a thing is of course just impossible. A good man's goodness, Jesus told his friends, can no more be hidden than a city that is built—Where?

4. Jesus one time described a man bringing a gift to be laid upon the altar in the temple (a good thing to do) and there re-

[Answers on page 38]

membering something that bothered him. What was it? And what did Jesus say that he ought to do about it?

5. Whatever else it is, all swearing and most of what we call "slang" is foolish and meaningless, a slipshod way of people who have never learned to use words carefully and rightly. About this loose, thoughtless kind of talk, Jesus once spoke severely. What did he say?

No. 4

One of the things about which Jesus talked often with his friends was the kingdom of heaven—or of God. He compared it to some things which they knew well. He told them some things about it that puzzled them but that to us, today, are clearer. Can you tell, in your own words, some of the things he said? For instance:

1. Do you remember how he compared the kingdom of heaven to a grain of mustard seed?

2. Some people of Jesus' time thought of his kingdom as a place, or as something which they could see coming—like a marching army. Jesus told them it was not like that. The kingdom of heaven was much nearer, in fact it was—Where?

3. In all the kingdoms of which history books tell, money has always been powerful. Jesus said that with him it was different. Just what did he say about rich men and his kingdom?

4. In the beatitudes (the "blesseds") Jesus said something about the kingdom of heaven and the poor in spirit. Can you remember what it was?

5. In his greatest sermon, Jesus spoke of the need of food and clothing but—How do they compare with the kingdom of God?

No. 5

Always people were asking Jesus questions. Sometimes honestly, because they really wished to know, sometimes dishonestly to "entangle him in his talk," and so undermine his popularity. Always Jesus answered wisely. The following questions call for five of his replies. These need not be given in his exact words.

1. After John the Baptist had lain long in prison, he began (not unnaturally) to be troubled and a little discouraged, even

[Answers on page 38]

doubting. Finally, he sent friends to Jesus asking, "Art thou he that should come, or do we look for another?" What did Jesus tell them?

2. Jesus once sat beside an ancient well talking with a woman who recognized him as a "prophet" and who instantly leaped to the conclusion that the great religious difference between them was that he thought God must be worshipped in Jerusalem, while her people believed he might be worshipped in a neighboring mountain. Jesus told her—What?

3. A lovable young man once came to Jesus, running, and asked, "Good Master, what shall I do to inherit eternal life?" What directions did Jesus give him?

4. A man deeply in earnest but puzzled, and perhaps afraid, once came to Jesus at night to learn more about his teaching. When Jesus told him one must be born again, he asked, "How can a man be born when he is old?" What did Jesus say?

5. The Jews hated their Roman masters and bitterly resented being a subject people. Having this in mind, certain clever enemies framed for Jesus a question his answer to which must, they felt sure, involve him in serious trouble: "Is it lawful to give tribute to Cæsar—or not?" What did Jesus say?

No. 6

Much of Jesus' teaching his hearers, even his disciples, found difficult. This was partly because it was so different from what they were used to and partly because they were humble men, unused to teaching of any sort. When they did not understand, they often came to him with their questions and he answered, sometimes directly, sometimes in stories that are called parables.

1. Jesus lived in a troubled time and clearly foresaw disaster for his country, distress for his followers. How could they avoid it? They wondered. So they asked him when these things would come to pass. What did he tell them?

2. To show the importance of being ready—ready for the demands of either life or death—Jesus told a story based upon the marriage customs of his day, a story of ten lamps and ten girls. Five of the girls he called wise and five foolish. What was it made the difference?

[Answers on pages 38–39]

3. How to get rid of the bad people in the world? A tyrant might say, "Why—kill them of course." But in one of his stories Jesus would seem to say, "No. You cannot destroy bad people without at the same time destroying much that is good." The story is about a wheat field, a farmer, his hired men and an enemy. Can you name it?

4. To give some idea of what "the end of the world" (or perhaps the end of each life) might be, Jesus described himself as sitting in judgment upon good men and bad, dividing them "as a shepherd divideth his sheep from the goats." On what basis was the division made?

5. Nearly all Jesus' stories were about everyday things. Once he described to his hearers something that every one of them must have seen a hundred times: a farmer sowing his field in the spring time. Perhaps just because it was so familiar, that story puzzled the disciples and they asked him for its meaning— What did he tell them?

No. 7

It was said of Jesus that the common people heard him gladly and one reason for it may well have been that there was never a story teller like him. He told the two most famous short stories in the world ("The Prodigal Son" and "The Good Samaritan") though both were of course much more than "just stories." And he told a number of others. Can you identify the following stories by what is here told about them?

1. One of the most dangerous things that can happen to any man is to get the idea that he is very, very good—much better than most men. Such a man Jesus told about as going up to the temple to pray—a strange prayer, mostly bragging. Can you tell any more of the story?

2. How much wages should a man be paid? That is of course a complicated question, not easy to answer. It all depends: upon the workman—the kind of work—and many other things. But one answer given by Jesus seems to be, "A man should be paid enough to live on." What story did he tell to illustrate this?

3. Some people, strangely enough, think of prayer not as a way of learning to know God but as a way of getting things and, if they ask for something six or seven times and fail to get it,

[Answers on page 39]

they may decide to stop. To show how foolish this idea was, Jesus told a rather amusing story about a poor woman who had a just grievance and—What happened?

4. The most important thing about any person is of course not what he owns, or even what he knows but what he *is*. Has he, as we sometimes say, a good character? To teach that that is more important than anything else, Jesus once told a story about a man whose business it was to buy gems. What is the story called?

5. How does a person, or a home, or a town become " good " ? How will the great, wicked world be transformed one day into God's kingdom? By hard work, you may say, but in another way too that we see every day and do not understand. What was Jesus' story about it?

No. 8

In all four of our lives of Jesus, we read much about the last meal that he ate with his disciples. All the following questions are about things that he said at that time. How many of them can you answer—in your own words?

1. Many times all the disciples had seen grape vines growing. How did Jesus compare himself and the disciples to a grape vine?

2. At the last supper, Jesus gave his disciples a " new commandment." What was it?

3. Jesus tried to prepare his friends for the coming separation. Can you remember anything he said about his Father's house, to which he was going?

4. Jesus knew that great trouble was going to come to his friends. He told them about it plainly, " In the world ye shall have tribulation." Then he added five of the most astonishing words he ever spoke. Can you remember them?

5. The last supper seems to have ended with a prayer in which Jesus asked his Father to watch over these friends whom he was leaving. Did he pray for any one else?

No. 9

1. In Mark's gospel, we read about how friends once brought a sick man to Jesus to be healed and, because of the crowd, let him down through a hole they made in the roof. Jesus healed

[Answers on pages 39–40]

him but first said something to him which enraged some of those who heard. What was it?

2. Jesus once said something about waste which, considering the circumstances, is a little startling. He had fed a multitude with a boy's lunch and then, turning to his disciples, he said—What?

3. An important part of Jesus' teaching was that there is something far more important than the things some people would call *most* important—food, clothing, shelter. He once told his disciples that he had meat to eat that they did not know about and then explained it by saying—What?

4. Did you ever hear of some dreadful thing that had happened and find yourself thinking, " Those people must have been very wicked, or that would not have happened to them " ? What did Jesus say about this?

5. Jesus once said something about the durability of his teaching, which should be most reassuring in a time when religion seems to be suffering terrible reverses. What was it?

No. 10

1. A part of Jesus' first preaching was almost identical with that of John the Baptist. What did he say that John had already been saying?

2. The story of Jesus' temptation in the wilderness tells us something as to the value of the Bible. In each reply to the tempter are found the same three words. What are they?

3. After Jesus had preached and taught elsewhere, he once went back to his home town where, on the Sabbath, he was asked to read the Scriptures in the synagogue. He read a passage from Isaiah (Esaias) and then said—What?

4. Among the beautiful and tender invitations which Jesus gave is one addressed especially to people who work hard, who " labor and are heavy laden." What was it?

5. Beside the cross, upon which Jesus hung dying, stood the two people who were probably dearest to him of any upon the earth. Thinking not of himself but of them, he spoke to them, saying—What?

[Answers on page 40]

No. 11

1. To be a follower of Jesus is a pleasant and happy thing but also (and always) it costs something. All good things do. Once a man told Jesus he wanted to follow him—would follow him anywhere. But Jesus said—What?

2. Jesus' disciples tried to save him time and strength, for during the years of his ministry he was a very busy man. When, for instance, people brought their children to him, they told them not to bother him that way. But Jesus, when he heard of it, was displeased and said ——?

3. Jesus needed (and still needs) helpers to carry to all people the good news he brought. Once, when walking by the sea of Galilee, he saw two brothers named Andrew and Simon and asked them to do—What?

4. Even his closest friends were slow to understand Jesus. Some day, they imagined, he would be crowned in Jerusalem and then they, who were ambitious and wanted to be " great," would be given important places in the government. What did Jesus tell them about it?

5. One time a man came to Jesus and asked him, " What is the first commandment of all? " What did Jesus tell him?

No. 12

1. Jesus was often criticized by enemies and by people who did not understand him. For one thing, they said that some of the people he went with were not " nice " people. What did Jesus say about it? Tell in your own words.

2. Jesus once said something that should bring happiness to any one who tries to follow him. Some one had told him his mother and brothers were outside. " Who are my mother and brothers? " he answered and then went on ——

3. One time in the temple, Jesus saw many people making large gifts and saw also one poor woman who made a very small gift. What did he tell his friends about it?

4. We hear a great deal in these times about our " rights " and we *should* think of them but other things are sometimes far more important. A man once asked Jesus to speak to his brother

[Answers on page 41]

about some property—he thought it ought to be divided. But Jesus said ——

5. Not only did Jesus command us to forgive our enemies, he showed us in his own life just what he meant for, when he hung upon the cross and looked down upon the men who had put him there, he offered what prayer?

ANSWERS

Section II
THINGS THAT JESUS SAID

No. 1

1. Compared with beauty of character, Jesus said, even royal garments are not worth thinking about. His exact words are: " Why take ye thought for raiment? Consider the lilies of the field . . . even Solomon in all his glory was not arrayed like one of these " (Matt. 6: 28–29).

2. " Love your enemies, bless them that curse you, do good to them that hate you, and pray for them which despitefully use you and persecute you " (Matt. 5: 44).

3. Jesus' advice was: " Go cheerfully, do more than he asks —even if the distance be two miles instead of one." " And whosoever shall compel you to go a mile, go with him twain " (Matt. 5: 41).

4. He said, in effect, if we watch constantly and carefully for our own faults, we will find our work pretty well cut out for us. His exact words are, " Judge not that ye be not judged " (Matt. 7: 1; but read the verses following).

5. " Therefore, all things whatsoever ye would that men should do unto you, do ye even so to them; for this is the law and the prophets " (Matt. 7: 12).

No. 2

1. That God, the perfect one, loves to give good things to those who ask him (Matt. 7: 8–11).

2. He gave more than one. The most outspoken is perhaps that in Matthew 6: 31–34.

3. " By their fruits ye shall know them " (Matt. 7: 16–20).

4. The narrow, difficult road, because it leads to life (Matt. 7: 13–14).
5. Salt (Matt. 5: 13).

No. 3

1. "Blessed are the peace makers, for they shall be called the children of God" (Matt. 5: 9).
2. "Blessed are ye, when men shall revile you, and persecute you, and shall say all manner of evil against you falsely for my sake" (Matt. 5: 11).
3. Upon a hill (Matt. 5: 14).
4. The man remembered a quarrel. Jesus said the first thing for him to do was to make up the quarrel. Then he could come back and present his gift (Matt. 5: 23–24).
5. "But let your communication be, Yea, yea, and, Nay, nay, for whatsoever is more than this cometh of evil" (Matt. 5: 37).

No. 4

1. As the tree grew from a tiny seed, so he said would the kingdom of heaven grow from a small beginning into something great and wonderful (Matt. 13: 31–32).
2. In their own hearts—if they would receive it (Luke 17: 21).
3. Not that no rich man could get in but that it would be harder for him. His money would be not a help but a hindrance (Mark 10: 24).
4. He said that the kingdom of heaven belonged to the poor in spirit, "those who felt their spiritual need" (Matt. 5: 3).
5. "The kingdom of God and his righteousness" should, he said, always come first. As for food—clothing—shelter—"Your heavenly father knoweth that ye have need of all these things" (Matt. 6: 33).

No. 5

1. He told and showed them what he was doing. In effect he said, "Judge for yourselves" (Matt. 11: 4–6).
2. The *place* of worship, Jesus told her, was of little importance. "The true worshippers shall worship the Father in spirit and in truth" (John 4: 21–23).

3. The young man was rich and apparently cared too much for his vast possessions. Jesus told him to sell them, give the money to the poor and " come, take up the cross and follow me " (Mark 10: 17–21).

4. Jesus told him that the new birth was not physical but something spiritual—" of water and the spirit " (John 3: 5–6).

5. He told them to show him a coin and, when they admitted that the " image and superscription " were Cæsar's, he said, in effect, " Very well then: give to Cæsar what is Cæsar's and to God what is God's " (Matt. 22: 15–22).

No. 6

1. Jesus told them certain signs of coming trouble would be just as clear as those of the seasons: but, as for the exact time of world calamity, no one knew, " not the angels in heaven but my Father only " (Matt. 24: 32–36).

2. The difference was their " staying power." The wise had brought extra oil and so were prepared to wait, with lighted lamps, longer than the others (Matt. 25: 1–13).

3. The story is of course that of the wheat and the tares (Matt. 13: 24–30).

4. He divided them on the basis of what they had done for others. " I was an hungered and ye gave me meat," etc. (Matt. 25: 31–46).

5. That the " seed " was his teaching: he went on to tell what happened to it after it had been " sowed " (Luke 8: 5–15).

No. 7

1. The parable of The Pharisee and the Publican (Luke 18: 10–14).

2. The parable of The Laborers and the Vineyard (Matt. 20: 1–16).

3. The parable of The Unjust Judge. Because the woman refused to be discouraged and kept on coming, her plea was answered (Luke 18: 2–5).

4. The parable of The Pearl of Great Price (Matt. 13: 45–46).

5. The parable of The Growing Seed. Goodness grows, and his kingdom will grow, Jesus taught, in the same familiar, mysterious way that a seed grows in the ground (Mark 4: 26–29).

No. 8

1. He said that he was the vine and they were the branches. His father was the "husbandman," the one who cared for and cultivated the vine (John 15: 5).

2. "Love one another. Just as I have loved you——" If they did, he said, people would know that they were really his followers (John 13: 34–35).

3. That it contained "many mansions" and that he was going there to prepare a place for them (John 14: 1–3).

4. "But be of good cheer." He wanted them to know that there are things far worse than "tribulations" (John 16: 33).

5. Yes, he prayed for *us*. ". . . for them also which shall believe on me through their word." ("Those who through their message come to believe on me") (John 17: 20).

No. 9

1. "Son, thy sins be forgiven thee" (Mark 2: 5).

2. "Gather up the fragments that remain, that nothing be lost" (John 6: 12).

3. "My meat is to do the will of him that sent me and to finish his work" (John 4: 34).

4. "Nay, but except ye repent, ye shall all likewise perish" (Luke 13: 1–5).

5. There are several passages. The most reassuring is perhaps "Heaven and earth shall pass away but my words shall not pass away" (Mark 13: 31).

No. 10

1. "Repent, for the kingdom of heaven is at hand" (Matt. 4: 17).

2. "It is written . . ." (Matt. 4: 4, 7, 10).

3. "This day is this Scripture fulfilled in your ears" (Luke 4: 21).

4. "Come unto me. . . . Take my yoke upon you and learn of me . . ." (Matt. 11: 28–30).

5. ". . . behold thy son. . . . Behold thy mother" (John 19: 26–27).

No. 11

1. That, though the foxes had holes and the birds nests, he himself had not "where to lay his head" (Matt. 8: 20).
2. Let the little children come, "for of such is the kingdom of God" (Mark 10: 14).
3. To come with him and be "fishers of men" (Mark 1: 17).
4. That the real way to become great was by being helpful to each other (Mark 9: 35; 10: 44).
5. That the first commandment was, "Thou shalt love the Lord thy God," and the second, "like unto it," was, "Thou shalt love thy neighbor as thyself" (Mark 12: 28–31).

No. 12

1. He said it was like finding fault with a doctor because he spent more time with sick people than with well ones (Mark 2: 16–17).
2. They are "whosoever shall do the will of God" (Mark 3: 35).
3. That her gift was really larger than all the others: the others had so much to give—she had so little (Mark 12: 41–44).
4. "Who made a judge or a divider over you?" (Luke 12: 13–14).
5. "Father, forgive them, for they know not what they do" (Luke 23: 34).

Section III
WHO SAID IT?

Some of the following quotations have been chosen because they are of so great import.

Some because the words (and the words only) are so familiar—the circumstances are often completely forgotten.

Some because it makes so great a difference who was the speaker.

No. 1

We do not really know the Bible, if we know only its words without knowing who spoke (or wrote) them and under what circumstances. That often makes all the difference in the world. By way of test, take the following quotations, all spoken (not written) by some Bible character. Who was it?

1. Choose ye this day whom ye will serve . . . but, as for me and my house, we will serve the Lord.
2. Thou comest to me with a sword and with a spear . . . ; but I come to thee in the name of the Lord of hosts.
3. Go ye into all the world and preach the gospel to every creature.
4. Though he slay me, yet will I trust in him.
5. We ought to obey God rather than man.

No. 2

A famous preacher once read his text (it is among the following quotations) and then startled his congregation by saying, "I thank God this is a lie." He had read it from the Bible but he had good reason for calling it what he did.

Can you tell by whom the following words, all recorded in the Bible, were spoken?

1. Am I my brother's keeper?

[Answers on page 46]

2. Shall not the judge of all the earth do right?
3. All that a man hath will he give for his life.
4. Thou art the man.
5. And who is my neighbor?

No. 3

1. Is thy servant a dog that he should do this thing?
2. No doubt ye are the people and wisdom will die with you.
3. There is no restraint to the Lord, to save by many or by few.
4. How long halt ye between two opinions? If the Lord be God, follow him; but if Baal, then follow him.
5. Are not Abanah and Pharpar, rivers of Damascus, better than all the waters of Israel?

No. 4

1. It is expedient that one man should die for the people and that the whole nation perish not.
2. What is truth?
3. Whosoever shall be chief among you, let him be your servant.
4. There is no God.
5. God is no respecter of persons.

No. 5

1. Behold to obey is better than sacrifice . . .
2. The Lord gave and the Lord hath taken away; blessed be the name of the Lord.
3. Love your enemies, bless them that curse you, do good to them that hate you.
4. Soul, thou hast much goods laid up for many years . . . take thine ease, eat, drink, and be merry.
5. In him (God) we live, and move, and have our being.

No. 6

1. Unstable as water, thou shalt not excel.
2. If a man die, shall he live again?

[Answers on pages 46–47]

3. Fear not, for they that be with us are more than they that be with them.

4. I will not leave you comfortless. I will come to you.

5. I have fought a good fight, I have finished my course, I have kept the faith.

No. 7

1. Let there be no strife, I pray thee, between thee and me ... for we are brethren.

2. And, as thy servant was busy here and there, he was gone.

3. We have made a covenant with death and with hell are we in agreement ... we have made lies our refuge and under falsehood have we hid ourselves.

4. I have sinned, in that I have betrayed innocent blood.

5. I am Alpha and Omega, the beginning and the end.

No. 8

1. The Lord watch between me and thee, when we are absent one from another.

2. Be not afraid of them. Remember the Lord.

3. Is there no balm in Gilead? Is there no physician there?

4. God is a spirit and they that worship him must worship him in spirit and in truth.

5. ... a lover of hospitality.

No. 9

1. I shall go to him but he shall not return to me.

2. But will God indeed dwell on the earth? Behold the heaven and the heaven of heavens cannot contain thee.

3. Can two walk together, except they be agreed?

4. He that findeth his life shall lose it.

5. (God) hath made of one blood all nations of men.

No. 10

1. My punishment is greater than I can bear.

2. Quit yourselves like men.

3. I shall go softly all my years.

4. The harvest truly is plenteous but the laborers are few.

5. Come over into Macedonia and help us.

[Answers on pages 47–49]

No. 11

1. Whoso sheddeth man's blood, by man shall his blood be shed.
2. There ariseth a little cloud out of the sea, like a man's hand.
3. Thou art weighed in the balances and found wanting.
4. The spirit truly is willing, but the flesh is weak.
5. When I have a convenient season, I will call for thee.

No. 12

1. Hast thou found me, O mine enemy?
2. Here am I. Send me.
3. The Sabbath was made for man, not man for the Sabbath.
4. I am the voice of one crying in the wilderness.
5. Be ye angry and sin not. Let not the sun go down upon your wrath.

[Answers on page 49]

ANSWERS

Section III
WHO SAID IT?

No. 1

1. Joshua, in his farewell address to his people (Joshua 24: 15).
2. David, answering the challenge of Goliath (I Sam. 17: 45).
3. Jesus: his final commission to his disciples (Mark 16: 15).
4. Job, expressing his confidence in God: after being badgered by his three " comforters " (Job 13: 15).
5. Peter (and the other apostles) when on trial before the council (Acts 5: 29).

No. 2

1. Cain, in replying to the Lord's question, " Where is thy brother? " (Gen. 4: 9).
2. Abraham. A rhetorical question addressed to the Lord (Gen. 18: 25).
3. Satan, in replying to the Lord's question, " Hast thou considered my servant Job? " (Job 2: 4).
4. The prophet Nathan, climaxing his accusation of King David, in his parable of The Ewe Lamb (II Sam. 12: 7).
5. " A certain lawyer," whose question led Jesus to tell the story of The Good Samaritan (Luke 10: 29).

No. 3

1. Hazael, when told by Elisha of the life he was destined to live (II Kings 8: 13).
2. Job, when the " comfort " of his friends had become particularly exasperating (Job 12: 2).

3. Jonathan, to his armor bearer, when they were about to make a sortie against the Philistines (I Sam. 14: 6).
4. Elijah, in his challenge to the people from Mount Carmel (I Kings 18: 21).
5. Naaman, the Syrian, when objecting to Elisha's cure for leprosy (II Kings 5: 12).

No. 4
1. Caiaphas (John 11: 50).
2. Pilate's question to Jesus. It was probably asked cynically (John 18: 38).
3. Jesus to his disciples (Matt. 20: 27).
4. The fool (hath said in his heart . . .) (Psalms 14: 1).
5. Peter to Cornelius, after his enlightening vision, in the home of Simon the tanner (Acts 10: 34).

No. 5
1. Samuel, in rebuking King Saul (I Sam. 15: 22).
2. Job, in the midst of his deluge of troubles (Job 1: 21).
3. Jesus, in the Sermon on the Mount (Matt. 5: 44).
4. The Rich Fool, in Jesus' parable of that name (Luke 12: 19).
5. Paul, in his sermon on Mars Hill (Acts 17: 28).

No. 6
1. Jacob: spoken of his first-born son, Reuben (Gen. 49: 4).
2. Job here asks the question asked and answered (in some fashion) by all religions (Job 14: 14).
3. Elisha to his frightened servant (II Kings 6: 16).
4. Jesus at the last supper with his disciples (John 14: 18).
5. Paul, writing to Timothy (II Tim. 4: 7).

No. 7
1. Abraham is speaking to Lot, when strife had developed between their herdsmen (Gen. 13: 8).
2. "A certain man of the sons of the prophets" says this in a story reproving King Ahab (I Kings 20: 40).

3. The prophet attributes these words to "scornful men that rule this people" (Isa. 28: 15).

4. Judas, as his tragedy approaches its climax (Matt. 27: 4).

5. In the Revelation, John gives us these words as from the lips of Jesus (Rev. 22: 13).

No. 8

1. Laban to Jacob (Gen. 31: 49). The two men were suspicious of each other and for them the words had a very different meaning from that which we commonly attach to them.

2. Nehemiah to some of his fearful and questioning associates (Neh. 4: 14).

3. Jeremiah 8: 22.

4. Jesus to the woman of Sychar (John 4: 24).

5. Paul, in writing to his young friend Titus, mentions this as one of the qualities which should be found in a bishop (overseer) (Titus 1: 8).

No. 9

1. David lamenting the death of the child born of his sin with Bathsheba (II Sam. 12: 23).

2. Solomon in his prayer dedicating the first temple (I Kings 8: 27).

3. One of the rhetorical questions of the prophet Amos (Amos 3: 3).

4. Jesus to his disciples (Matt. 10: 39).

5. Paul in his address to the Athenians (Acts 17: 26).

No. 10

1. Cain, speaking to Jehovah (Gen. 4: 13).

2. Amplified, the quotation reads, " Be strong and quit yourselves like men, O ye Philistines " (I Sam. 4: 9). It was evidently a word passed about among the troops as they went out to battle with Israel.

3. It is a part of the "writing of Hezekiah . . . when he . . . was recovered of his sickness " (Isa. 38: 15).

4. Jesus, when he saw the multitude, " scattered abroad, as sheep having no shepherd " (Matt. 9: 37).

5. The man of Macedonia, whom Paul saw in a vision of the night (Acts 16: 9).

No. 11

1. Jehovah, speaking to Noah after the flood (Gen. 9: 6).
2. Elijah's servant, when sent to look for signs of the coming rain (I Kings 18: 44).
3. Daniel interpreting the handwriting upon the wall of Belshazzar's banquet hall (Dan. 5: 27).
4. Jesus, to the three drowsy disciples in Gethsemane (Mark 14: 38).
5. Felix, the governor, after hearing Paul reason " of righteousness, temperance and judgment to come " (Acts 24: 25).

No. 12

1. King Ahab, in speaking to the prophet Elijah (I Kings 21: 20).
2. The prophet Isaiah in accepting his commission (Isa. 6: 8).
3. Jesus, replying to critics who accused him of profaning the Sabbath by performing on that day a miracle of healing (Mark 2: 27).
4. John the Baptist quoting Isaiah 40: 3 (John 1: 23).
5. Paul in his letter to the Ephesians—one of many items of good advice (Eph. 4: 26).

Section IV
BIBLE ACQUAINTANCES

It would of course have been easy to compile a list of Bible characters not readily identifiable. To Bible readers most of the following will be familiar. They are termed "acquaintances" rather than friends, since as friends some of them, alas! would not have been desirable.

To those wishing to keep score: a correct answer, after reading the first statement, counts 100; after the second, 75; after the third, 50; after the fourth, 25.

No. 1

1. Born in Ur of the Chaldees, I left my home-land, taking with me all that I possessed, to become, religiously as well as geographically, an explorer of new frontiers.
2. A wide and fruitful land was promised to me and to my children but though "rich in cattle, in silver, and in gold," I myself never possessed it.
3. Living among a people who practiced human sacrifice, I had revealed to me a form of worship more humane and acceptable.
4. I am held in reverence alike by Jews, Christians and Mohammedans.

Who am I?

No. 2

1. An Egyptian maid servant, I was so persecuted by my mistress that I once fled from her into the wilderness.
2. There the angel of the Lord found me and persuaded me to return.
3. He promised that I should become the mother of a great

[Answers on page 61]

people but said of my son that "his hand will be against every man and every man's hand against him."

4. Because of my mistress's continued jealousy, I knew exile, suffering and despair but lived to see the fulfillment of what had been promised me.

Who am I?

No. 3

1. When my kinsman, Abraham, left Ur of the Chaldees, I accompanied him.

2. We both had many flocks and herds and, when friction developed between our herdsmen and it seemed best to separate, he generously gave me my choice of grazing country.

3. I chose the plain of Jordan, as being well watered, and pitched my tent toward Sodom.

4. In a foray of neighboring kings, my household and I were made prisoners but were rescued by Abraham.

Who am I?

No. 4

1. I was "a soothsayer of Peor on the Euphrates," called in professionally by the king of Moab to curse the Israelites newly come out of Egypt.

2. Instead of cursing them, what I actually did was, again and again, to bless them and foretell their future greatness.

3. My employer was naturally enraged. I explained that I would gladly oblige him but could speak only such oracles as were delivered to me.

4. Sorely tempted by his rich gifts, I finally worked out a compromise, by which I thought I could "serve God and Mammon." One result was my own death.

Who am I?

No. 5

1. The lifelong friend of a great soldier, he and I took part in our youth in a famous scouting expedition.

2. Our associates denounced our counsel of immediate invasion, absurdly declaring that, in comparison with the stature of our enemies, we were like grasshoppers.

[Answers on page 61]

3. Of that whole reconnoitering expedition, we two were the only ones who survived to enter and possess the land we had explored.

4. At four score and five, feeling myself as strong as in middle life, the only reward which I asked for my service was a new and difficult task—a conquest still to be made.

Who am I?

No. 6

1. Left a young and childless widow, I found strength and consolation in my love for my husband's mother.

2. When, leaving my own country (Moab), she returned to her own land, I went with her, declaring that her people should be my people and her God my God.

3. Alien though I was, I was kindly received in her home town and contracted there, with her full approval, a second marriage.

4. A son was born to me and, years later, one of my great-grandsons rose to be the best loved king of the people who in my sorrow had been kind to me.

Who am I?

No. 7

1. I was a giant and the sight of me should have been enough to strike terror to any heart—let alone that of a boy.

2. Nevertheless, when I asked for a champion from the opposing army, it was a boy who came out to fight me.

3. I was armed with shield, helmet, sword and spear.

4. His arms were a sling and five smooth stones. One was all he needed.

Who am I?

No. 8

1. Eldest son of the first king who ever ruled over Israel and popular with the people, I myself never came to the throne.

2. Some might call me great in my own right but I am known to history chiefly because of my friendship for the man whom I might well have regarded as my rival.

[Answers on page 61]

3. All my life my people were at war with a powerful enemy and I myself was finally slain by them in battle.
4. An elegy, "The Song of the Bow," was composed upon my death by a royal poet.
Who am I?

No. 9

1. Born into a royal family, I suffered as a young man from two grave handicaps: my father was too lenient with me and I was strikingly handsome.
2. No king ever ruled our people who was more beloved than my father, yet, when I rose in rebellion against him, I almost succeeded in dethroning him.
3. Though he gave strict orders that I should in no wise be harmed, his commander-in-chief slew me in cold blood, when I was defenceless.
4. My father's lament for me has become the classic example of parental grief over a wayward child.
Who am I?

No. 10

1. I was closely related to Israel's first king and was "captain of his host."
2. After his death in the battle of Mount Gilboa, I set up one of his sons as a puppet king, I myself being the real power behind the throne.
3. When defeated in battle by Joab, David's commander-in-chief, I sought a negotiated peace that would have been favorable to David.
4. At this Joab became jealous and apprehensive and by him I was treacherously murdered.
5. It has been said of me (truly I fear) that, while brave and capable, I was "destitute of all lofty ideas of morality or religion."
Who am I?

No. 11

1. I was a prophet of God and a confidential adviser to King David.

[Answers on page 61]

2. When he was planning to build a temple to Jehovah, it was my task to tell him that this was not to be.

3. When he was old and the sceptre was slipping from his senile hand, I was able to secure the succession of Solomon.

4. I wrote a life of my hero-king, which however has not come down to modern times (I Chron. 29: 29).

5. I am best known for my rebuke to the king, conveyed in the parable of The Ewe Lamb (II Sam. 12: 1–7).

Who am I?

No. 12

1. I built the first temple and my prayer at its dedication is one of the masterpieces of sacred literature.

2. Of me it is recorded that I spoke three thousand proverbs and that my songs were a thousand and five.

3. My great reputation for wisdom was belied by my statecraft, the magnificence of my reign proving shallow and deceptive.

4. The book of Ecclesiastes claims me as its author—or hero.

Who am I?

No. 13

1. I succeeded a royal father, who had a great—though perhaps undeserved—reputation for wisdom. (I certainly inherited little of it.)

2. When, at my coronation, an influential group sought a promise that my rule would be milder than his, I took three days in which to weigh the matter.

3. During this interval, I consulted with my father's counsellors and with the young men of my own generation.

4. Acting on the advice of the young men, I told the deputation that my rule would be one of unexampled harshness.

5. The result, as any one might have anticipated, was a division of the kingdom and border warfare that lasted for years.

Who am I?

No. 14

1. My father's name was Nebat and I appear first in biblical history as a "labor boss" under King Solomon.

[Answers on page 61]

2. The prophet Ahijah solemnly assured me that one day I would rule over ten of the twelve tribes of my people.

3. Seeking to anticipate the time of this prophecy, I incurred the suspicion of the king and was obliged to fly for my life into Egypt.

4. When Solomon died and his foolish son came to the throne, I was able to take advantage of the situation and set up the so-called "northern kingdom," with my capital at Samaria.

5. I regarded it as politically unwise to allow my people to worship Jehovah in Jerusalem and, in the sacred writings, my name is often followed by the opprobrious words "who made Israel to sin."

Who am I?

No. 15

1. Nothing is known of my birth or parentage, save that I am sometimes referred to as "the Tishbite."

2. I foretold to King Ahab a drought of unexampled duration.

3. Felix Mendelssohn made my story the subject of one of his greatest musical compositions.

4. In a contest with the priests of Baal, upon Mount Carmel, I was completely victorious but fled when threatened by Queen Jezebel.

Who am I?

No. 16

1. I had the misfortune to own a valuable piece of property, desired by a rich and powerful neighbor.

2. He made me a proposition which you might consider fair, even generous.

3. When I refused it, he was bitterly disappointed, seeing which his wife took matters into her own hands.

4. The result was my judicial murder, a crime which brought a scathing rebuke from the prophet Elijah.

Who am I?

No. 17

1. One day, when I was ploughing with twelve yoke of oxen

[Answers on page 61]

in one of my father's fields, a prophet passed and cast his mantle upon me.

2. Recognizing this as a call from God, I followed him and, after his translation, became recognized as his successor.

3. I came to have great influence, not only among kings and captains but also over a religious body known as "the sons of the prophets."

4. My ministry covers a period of something like fifty years (B. C. 855–798).

Who am I?

No. 18

1. Sent by the prophet Elisha, a young man came, at the risk of his life, to tell me that I was to be king of Israel.

2. Backed by fellow captains, I rose at once in rebellion against my master, King Joram.

3. My rebellion was bloody and successful.

4. Though I lived in a time when motor vehicles were undreamed of, my name has become a synonym for reckless driving (II Kings 9: 20).

Who am I?

No. 19

1. I lived in sad and troubled times, and it is not strange that I am sometimes called "the weeping prophet."

2. No other sacred writer, declares a modern scholar, has described his life, both public and private, with such intimacy as did I, in my "prophetic autobiography."

3. A patriot, making a stubborn, lifelong fight against corruption and demagoguery, I was at last carried away, an exile from a ruined country, into Egypt, where my life ends in obscurity and oblivion.

4. Nevertheless, my message is not one of utter hopelessness, for I discovered and proclaimed that life has greater values than national glory and prosperity.

Who am I?

No. 20

1. No mention of me occurs in the Old Testament outside the book which bears my name.

2. This was long considered an allegory, but it is now recognized that, as a part of my prophecies, I recorded the story of my own life.

3. Through the wreck of my domestic happiness, I came to a fuller comprehension of the yearning love of God for his people.

4. Living as I did in a period of rapidly advancing decay, I bid Israel find the heart of religion not in ceremony or in formal sacrifices but in kindness.

Who am I?

No. 21

1. A herdsman and a dresser of sycamores, my home was in the little village of Tekoa, not far from Bethlehem.

2. Though neither a (professional) prophet nor the son of a prophet, I became a spokesman for Jehovah, and my words are the earliest prophetic writings that have come down to the present times.

3. Humble as were my surroundings, I was by no means ignorant of the life of my people, and my denunciations of social injustices are among the most scathing ever uttered.

4. With me " prophecy breaks away on its true lines, individual, direct, responsible to none save God."

Who am I?

No. 22

1. At the beginning of the Christian era, I was the most powerful man in the world.

2. Yet my name is mentioned but once in the four gospels and then only by way of accurately placing a date.

3. I rose to power because adopted by an uncle who was, perhaps, the most famous dictator of all time.

4. The fact that divine honors were claimed for me (and my successors) and were refused by members of the Christian church led to some of the early persecutions.

Who am I?

No. 23

1. I am described as the fulfillment of an ancient prophecy: " the voice of one crying in the wilderness."

[Answers on page 61]

2. My preaching was in the desert, much of it was denunciatory, yet so deeply were the people moved that the whole countryside flocked out to hear me.

3. From prison I sent messengers to my Great Successor, asking, "Art thou he that cometh, or look we for another?"

4. My death was due to a king's rash promise, the art of a dancing girl and a woman's implacable hatred.

Who am I?

No. 24

1. The Master described me as "an Israelite indeed, in whom is no guile."

2. This in spite of my rather supercilious question, "Can anything good come out of Nazareth?"

3. Wisely taking the advice of a friend, to "come and see," I was amply convinced.

4. I appear (it is believed) among the twelve, under the patronymic of Bartholomew.

Who am I?

No. 25

1. We were sisters living in a suburb of Jerusalem, in a home often visited by the Master.

2. Of one of us it was said that she was troubled and overanxious about household cares.

3. Of the other, that she had chosen "the good part, which shall not be taken away from her."

4. Nevertheless, we were both devoted followers, and in our time of greatest need, the Master brought us comfort and help.

Who were we?

No. 26

1. I had two handicaps: (a) I was short of stature and (b) all my countrymen despised me because of my job.

2. But then—I was rich and influential. Why should I care?

3. I had heard of Jesus, the prophet of Galilee, and, when he came to my city, I climbed a tree to catch a glimpse of him.

4. He stopped beneath the tree—called me by name—said

[Answers on page 61]

he would like to go to my home. The result was a complete change in my whole life.

Who am I?

No. 27

1. I made my home with two sisters in the village of Bethany, not far from Jerusalem.
2. The Prophet of Galilee was often a guest in our home and it is recorded that he spoke of me to his disciples as " our friend."
3. I was the subject of what most people would probably call his greatest miracle.
4. Far from convincing his enemies, this miracle made them the more hostile against him and also against me.

Who am I?

No. 28

1. My name is not recorded in the gospels but I may be identified by the name of the village from which I went one noon day to draw a pitcher of water.
2. At the well curb I met a man from whom (being a Samaritan) I expected nothing more than a contemptuous glance but he asked me for a drink of water.
3. I recognized him as a " prophet " and we fell to talking of religion.
4. So wonderful were the things he said that I found myself asking, " Is not this the Christ? "

Who am I?

No. 29

1. My brother James and I were partners with Peter and Andrew in the fishing business.
2. When I became a follower of the Master, I was one of the three who were most intimate with him.
3. My fellow disciples were angry with me because my mother sought special favors for my brother and me from the Master's hand.
4. There was " a saying among the brethren " that I should not die but this was due to a misunderstanding of something said by the Master after his resurrection.

Who am I?

[Answers on page 61]

No. 30

1. I was one of the twelve friends who were most intimate with Jesus and, in John's gospel, my name is followed by the words, "which is called Didymus."

2. When the Master was bent upon going into grave danger, I proposed to my fellow disciples that we should go with him, "that we may die with him."

3. When told of the resurrection, I was skeptical, declaring that I would believe nothing short of the evidence of my own senses.

4. This was given me and I was fully convinced.

Who am I?

[Answers on page 61]

ANSWERS
Section IV
BIBLE ACQUAINTANCES

No. 1. Abraham.
No. 2. Hagar.
No. 3. Lot.
No. 4. Balaam.
No. 5. Caleb.
No. 6. Ruth.
No. 7. Goliath.
No. 8. Jonathan.
No. 9. Absalom.
No. 10. Abner, the son of Ner.
No. 11. Nathan.
No. 12. King Solomon.
No. 13. Rehoboam.
No. 14. Jeroboam.
No. 15. Elijah.
No. 16. Naboth.
No. 17. Elisha.
No. 18. Jehu.
No. 19. The Prophet Jeremiah.
No. 20. The Prophet Hosea.
No. 21. The Prophet Amos.
No. 22. Cæsar Augustus.
No. 23. John the Baptist.
No. 24. Nathanael.
No. 25. Mary and Martha.
No. 26. Zacchæus.
No. 27. Lazarus.
No. 28. The woman of Sychar.
No. 29. John the Apostle.
No. 30. Thomas.

Section V
BOOKS OF THE BIBLE

To identify all the books of the Bible on the basis of a few general statements like the following would demand a much larger amount of specialized information than the average reader can be supposed to have. The following quiz covers therefore less than half of the total number of Bible books.

If the guessing forms a contest, score may be kept thus: a correct answer, after reading the first statement, counts 100; after reading the second, 80; after the third, 60; after the fourth, 40; after the fifth, 20.

No. 1

1. Its earlier chapters deal with the history of primeval mankind and one ancient manuscript entitles it the "Book of Origins."

2. The bulk of it consists of "a simple narrative history of the Hebrew forefathers—a glorified picture of their shepherd life—tales among the noblest literature that has survived to us from the past" (Breasted).

3. These records are also called "the earliest example of historical writing in prose which we have inherited from any people" (Breasted).

4. It contains the most popular "success story" of all time; that of a slave boy who became prime minister of the greatest nation then in existence.

5. While often termed the "first book of Moses," practically all modern Bible scholars agree that it is a compilation from many sources.

No. 2

1. It has been called "a prophetic law book," because fifteen of its chapters contain a code of laws.

[Answers on page 75]

2. One of its passages, frequently called the Shema from its first word, "has been for many ages the first bit of the Bible which Jewish children have learned to say and to read."

3. It brought to the people for whom it was written a new message about God.

4. It contains a striking "song," which reflects a time when the nation was oppressed but when the poet saw deliverance not far away.

5. It is the last in a series of books known to scholars as the Pentateuch.

No. 3

1. It is the last in the series of books known to scholars as the Hexateuch.

2. It presents the biography of a soldier who led his people in a war of conquest.

3. He was inaugurated into his position by Israel's great law-giver.

4. One of his earliest and most dramatic victories was the capture of the city of Jericho.

5. In the last chapter of the book he appears as an old man, pleading with his people to remain faithful to the God of their fathers.

No. 4

1. It covers a period when "there was no king in Israel; every man did that which was right in his own eyes."

2. Its ever recurring theme is the nation oppressed because of sin, deliverance through a champion raised up by Jehovah, relapse into idolatry.

3. It contains a number of highly picturesque and sometimes gruesome stories. For instance, a strong man carries away the gates of a city, a father offers his daughter as a human sacrifice, a chieftain at the head of three hundred men makes a night attack upon a huge army and puts it to flight.

4. While it pictures political relations which were disordered to the point of actual civil war, the general trend of events is toward a greater unification of the people.

[Answers on page 75]

5. In its setting forth of the life and customs of a primitive people, the book has great historic and archeological value.

No. 5

1. It is one of the so-called biblical idylls, its theme being "a friendship between two women and the grand climax to which all is working . . . the birth of a baby."
2. It contains what is perhaps the most famous and beautiful pledge of devotion in all literature.
3. It reveals the fact that King David's heritage was not purely Hebrew, but contained a strain of Moabitish blood.
4. A great Bible teacher says of it: "(It) has done more to help us live over again in remote antiquity than all the heroic achievements of Joshua and Judges put together."
5. It is one of the two books of the Bible having a woman's name for its title.

No. 6

1. It would seem, from its title, to be a biography in two volumes.
2. However, the "hero" dies before the end of volume one, and in volume two his name is not once mentioned.
3. It contains some of the finest stories of adventure to be found in sacred or secular literature, one of them being the well-known story of a boy's fight with a giant.
4. One of its minor episodes is the story of a friendship between two young men, which has become proverbial.
5. The real theme of the book is the firm establishment of the Jewish kingdom. At its beginning, the Hebrews are dominated by the Philistines. At its conclusion, their independence has been triumphantly secured.

No. 7

1. Its author, described as a priest and "a scribe of the law," was a stalwart reformer during the governorship of Nehemiah.
2. Not a resident of Palestine, he brought a company of returning exiles thither at a time when Babylonia was the real center of Jewish wealth and culture.

3. Part of the book describes their four months' journey to Jerusalem.

4. The book also describes the rebuilding and rededication of the temple and the re-establishment of Jehovah's worship.

5. While a commanding figure, the writer also appears at times as austere and harsh. It is claimed for him that "he is the true founder of Judaism."

No. 8

1. The book consists in large measure of extracts from the personal memoirs of a courtier who lived about 459 B. C.

2. Distressed by reports of conditions in Jerusalem, he sought and obtained a temporary leave of absence from his position at the court of Artaxerxes and went to the assistance of his people.

3. At Jerusalem, despite opposition both open and secret, he rebuilt the city wall and introduced many governmental and religious reforms.

4. For some years he remained as governor of the province, under Persia, returning later to the court. Later still, he paid a second official visit to Jerusalem.

5. His personality is singularly attractive; a courageous, fervently patriotic and gifted man of action, "well versed in the ways of the world and well equipped to meet difficult situations."

No. 9

1. The heroine of the book is a beautiful young Jewess, who becomes queen of Persia in a time of dangerous crisis for her people.

2. Her success in saving them from massacre is due chiefly to a wise, old cousin, in whose home she was reared.

3. In the end, the "villain" of the story, who had plotted the massacre, suffers the identical fate which he had prepared for this relative.

4. The personnel and the exciting character of the events remind one of some of the Arabian Nights stories.

5. In the ten chapters of the book, the name of God is not once mentioned.

[Answers on page 75]

No. 10

1. Its theme is one of the great problems of all religions: why should suffering ever come to the just and the innocent?
2. A familiar passage, "I know that my redeemer liveth," gave Handel the words for one of the most beautiful solos in his *Messiah*.
3. Its literary form is that of a drama having prologue and epilogue; and more than once in recent years it has been so presented by students of religious drama.
4. The chief characters of the *dramatis personæ* are the protagonist, a group of friends who came to console with and accuse him, and God, who speaks out of a whirlwind. (Satan is a character in the prologue.)
5. The story is that of a man rich, prosperous, happy, and deserving, who is overtaken by utter ruin which, his friends assure him, must be because of some fault of his own. In the end his good fortune is restored to him.

No. 11

1. It is a collection of lyrics, which has been called the hymn book of the Jewish people. It has also served as the only hymn book for a number of Christian sects.
2. The themes of these lyrics offer great variety, from pompous ritual and national pæan to the cry of a solitary soul in the dark.
3. The authorship of many of them is ascribed to King David.
4. Dr. Henry Van Dyke said that three great qualities distinguish this book: (1) Deep and genuine love of nature; (2) a passionate sense of the beauty of holiness; (3) intense joy in God.
5. "Probably no book of the Old Testament has exercised a more profound and extensive influence over succeeding ages."

No. 12

1. The title of the book is commonly given as "—or the Preacher."
2. It has been called "a miscellany of wisdom—essays,

strings of disconnected brevities—maxims, epigrams, unit proverbs."

3. More familiar quotations come from it than from any other book of equal length in the whole Bible.

4. It contains the most familiar (and probably the most beautiful) description of old age to be found in any literature.

5. Its "hero" (some would say its author) is King Solomon.

No. 13

1. A colorful, dramatic poem, rich in Oriental imagery, which early commentators confidently affirmed was written by King Solomon.

2. Modern Bible scholars contend that there is no need to interpret the title as implying that Solomon was the author. "The words might equally refer to the fact that he is the hero of the poem."

3. Reading into it a deeply symbolic and spiritual meaning, the translators of the King James Version give it chapter synopses which the translators of the Revised Version omitted.

4. Its theme is the celebration of pure, conjugal love and "to some readers," says one modern literary critic, "it may seem that nothing more spiritual need be desired."

No. 14

1. A great book of world literature, as well as one of the greatest of prophecies, written partly in poetry and partly in prose, it bears the name of one author, though most biblical scholars believe it contains other, anonymous, prophecies "of many prophets living at different periods."

2. The author received his call early in life, "in the year that King Uzziah died." His public career covered a period of more than forty years.

3. The British novelist Arnold Bennett, in his essay on "Literary Taste," chose a passage from this prophecy (that beginning, "Comfort ye, comfort ye my people . . .") as an example of supremely great literature.

4. It furnished words for some of the best known and most

[Answers on page 75]

beautiful choruses of Handel's *Messiah:* among them "Unto us a Child is Born" and "All We like Sheep have Gone Astray."

5. It contains the most familiar of all prophecies of coming World Peace. + of The Messiah .

No. 15

1. From his name we derive a common noun, meaning an utterance of grief or sorrow.

2. His (ideal) portrait by Michael Angelo, upon the ceiling of the Sistine Chapel at Rome, is said to be one of the greatest figures ever painted.

3. He has given us many familiar Bible quotations: "Peace, peace; when there is no peace;" "Is there no balm in Gilead?"; "Can the Ethiopian change his skin, or the leopard his spots?"

4. Born at Anathoth, a little town near Jerusalem, he lived through a time of great international strife, prophesying reluctantly but resolutely, his ministry a protracted martyrdom.

5. Foreseeing national overthrow, "he strove to teach his people that each must regard his own heart as a temple,—which would endure long after (Jehovah's) temple in Jerusalem had crashed into ruin" (Breasted).

No. 16

1. A member of the Jewish priesthood, he was carried into captivity about 600 B. C. and lived for years, consoling and teaching his fellow exiles, upon the banks of the river Chebar in Babylonia.

2. His most characteristic literary form is "emblem prophecy . . . a transitional stage in the development of the modern text and sermon."

3. Many of his emblems are strikingly vivid: a mimic siege carried out in great detail, a valley of dry bones, a wheel within a wheel, cedar branches, eagles, a cauldron.

4. Two such were the inspiration of well-known Negro spirituals.

5. The prophet had the disheartening experience of seeing his utterances valued for their high literary quality, "as a very lovely song of one that hath a pleasant voice, and can play on an instrument," while his rebukes and admonitions were ignored.

[Answers on page 75]

No. 17

1. The original of the book, as we have it, is written in two languages. It begins and ends in Hebrew, with an insert of some length in Aramaic.
2. It bears the name of one who, as a captive in a foreign land, attained a position of great power and influence in the then dominant court of the world.
3. His influence there made him a subject of jealousy and conspiracy, and it is explained that, once at least, he was in grave peril of his life.
4. The relevation with which the book closes is a conspicuous example of apocalyptic literature.
5. While the stories of the book have delighted many generations of children, "its salient ideas," to quote an eminent literary critic, "have been absorbed into the common heritage of poetic associations which make the groundwork of literary speech."

No. 18

1. The story is that of a prophet commanded to foretell the doom of one of the greatest cities of antiquity.
2. Feeling, apparently, that he might get beyond the jurisdiction of Jehovah, he took ship for a distant port.
3. At sea he underwent great perils but did not escape the charge laid upon him.
4. When his preaching received far greater (and more favorable) attention than he had anticipated, he was bitterly disappointed.
5. The miraculous (or allegorical) element in the story has obscured its important teaching.

No. 19

1. It is classified as one of the anonymous prophecies; the name given in our Bible meaning simply "my messenger."
2. When the disciples asked Jesus, "How is it that the scribes say that Elijah must first come?" they were referring to a prophecy contained in this book, the fulfillment of which was confidently expected in their time.

[Answers on page 75]

3. It contains the familiar words, "Then they that feared the Lord spake often one with another—and a book of remembrance was written."

4. Another familiar passage is the source of the children's Sunday School hymn, *Precious Jewels*.

5. The theme of the book is "a call for social and religious purification, and a pledge that this messenger of the Lord will surely come," a theme which makes peculiarly appropriate the place assigned it in our Bible.

No. 20

1. It begins with a genealogy which traces the descent of its subject back to Abraham.

2. Its (traditional) author held office under the Roman government and was despised for it by his fellow countrymen.

3. It contains our most complete report of the greatest sermon of all time.

4. The writer shows that he is deeply interested in the fulfillment of prophecy.

5. To it we owe our only account of the visit of the Magi.

No. 21

1. A biography of twenty-four chapters, the work of a widely-travelled, Gentile physician.

2. It deals more fully with the birth and childhood of its subject than does any of the three similar narratives.

3. A preface addresses the book to a certain Theophilus, believed to have been a Roman citizen of rank.

4. To its author we owe also the book of The Acts of the Apostles.

5. He has been described as "the most literary and versatile" of the four evangelists.

No. 22

1. One of the lives of Jesus, it makes no mention of lepers, demoniacs, publicans, scribes, or Sadducees, nor does it contain a single parable.

2. Omitting any reference to the birth of Jesus at Bethlehem,

[Answers on page 75]

it begins with an introduction of eighteen verses, which is one of the masterpieces of sacred literature.

3. Five of its twenty-one chapters are taken up with an account of what took place at the Last Supper.

4. While its authorship has been the subject of much controversy, many now believe that it was written at Ephesus by one called "the Presbyter."

5. Some one has said of it that "no other book of the Bible has left such a mark at the same time upon the profoundest Christian thinkers and upon simple-minded believers at large."

No. 23

1. The author was a liberally educated and widely travelled professional man, already represented in the biblical canon by a supremely great biography.

2. Its time is the first century and its scene the Roman Empire. The narrative takes us from people to people, from province to province, and finally leaves us in the capital city itself.

3. It may be said to have two heroes: one a Galilean fisherman, with little or no formal education, the other a scholarly university man, a Roman citizen, and a pupil of the famous Gamaliel.

4. Its opening shows us Christianity as an obscure, struggling Jewish sect. In its last pages it is firmly implanted at a score of strategic spots and well on its way to become the dominant religion of the western world.

5. It contains a description of a voyage and shipwreck unmatched by the best in *Robinson Crusoe*.

No. 24

1. The book is made up of two volumes of letters, bearing the name not of the man who wrote them, but of the man who received them.

2. He (the recipient) was a native of Lystra, the son of a Greek father and a Jewish mother. He had worked hard and travelled widely in spreading the gospel among the Gentiles.

3. Later he had become a young minister, heavily weighted with responsibilities. Thus, naturally, much of the book is made

[Answers on page 75]

up of an older and more experienced friend's advice for meeting his problems. It is rightly described as a "pastoral epistle."

4. The writer, who was perhaps the greatest of the early Christian leaders, addresses the recipient as "my dearly beloved son," although there was no blood relationship between them.

5. The last part of the book would seem to have been written from prison and in anticipation of a death sentence; nevertheless, it is triumphant, almost exultant in tone.

No. 25

1. An intimate and beautiful private letter, it is sent by the hand of a runaway slave.

2. The addressee is the master from whom the slave has escaped.

3. It requests that the slave be taken back "no longer as a servant but as a brother beloved."

4. The writer, at the time of the writing, appears to have been a prisoner in Rome.

5. The letter contains a pun upon the name of its bearer.

No. 26

1. It is an anonymous letter addressed to a whole people.

2. It seeks to convince them of the supreme high priesthood of a number of their race.

3. Its authorship has been assigned by various scholars, modern and medieval, to Paul, Luke, Barnabas, Apollos and Clement of Rome.

4. The writer presents, with great rhetorical skill, "the final truths of the Christian religion in their world wide relations."

5. One of its chapters (the eleventh) might be described as a Jewish Hall of Fame.

No. 27

1. Because it emphasizes "works" rather than "faith," Martin Luther called it "an epistle of straw."

2. It "stands apart from all the other epistles of the New Testament" in being closely related to the Wisdom Literature, an example of which is "Ecclesiasticus" in the Apocrypha.

3. Its main purpose was to encourage consistency of life and a firm endurance of persecution, which it does in a series of precepts and brief essays.

4. Its author, who was the "bishop" of the church at Jerusalem, seems to have regarded Christianity as a sect of Judaism rather than a separate religion. At any rate, he himself remained through life an orthodox Jew.

5. While describing himself as "a servant of God and of the Lord Jesus Christ," he is believed to have been the Lord's brother.

No. 28

1. Three brief letters (one of them the shortest book in the Bible) all known to us by the name of their author.

2. Of the first it has been said: "The style is simple but baffling. The sentences are easy for a child to read, their meaning is difficult for a wise man to analyze."

3. The letters lay emphasis "on love, on obedience, on fellowship with the Father and the Son, and the inestimable importance of maintaining and abiding in the truth."

4. The second letter is to "the elect lady and her children." (An address which has led to much speculation.) The third is to a personal friend, "Gaius, the beloved, whom I love in the truth."

5. Robert Browning's poem, "A Death in the Desert," describes what might have been the passing of the author of these letters.

No. 29

1. A letter of one chapter, its writer (perhaps a brother of the Master) contributed nothing else to the New Testament.

2. It is addressed to a church, or circle of churches, the geographical location of which is not known with certainty.

3. It consists of a solemn and scathing arraignment of false teachers and a warning to the faithful not to be misled.

4. It is not often read from our pulpits but its last two verses, beginning, "Now, unto him that is able to keep you from falling," is one of the most familiar of benedictions.

5. It is next to the last book in the Bible.

[Answers on page 75]

No. 30

1. While not listed among the epistles, this book was evidently intended for seven churches, to each of which a message of commendation or rebuke is sent.

2. It abounds in puzzling imagery and symbolism and has probably been more diversely interpreted than any other book in the Bible. Especially has it always appealed to the "lunatic fringe" of interpreters.

3. It contains what has been regarded as a curse upon any one who shall either add to or subtract from its contents.

4. No other book ever written has given a picture of the future life so revealing, alluring, and comforting; a city in which shall be gathered all nations, kindreds, and tongues; of unexampled beauty, without sin, without sorrow, lighted only by the splendor of God.

5. It was the last book written by John.

[Answers on page 75]

ANSWERS

Section V
BOOKS OF THE BIBLE

No. 1. The Book of Genesis.
No. 2. The Book of Deuteronomy.
No. 3. The Book of Joshua.
No. 4. The Book of Judges.
No. 5. The Book of Ruth.
No. 6. I and II Samuel.
No. 7. The Book of Ezra.
No. 8. The Book of Nehemiah.
No. 9. The Book of Esther.
No. 10. The Book of Job.
No. 11. The Book of Psalms.
No. 12. The Book of Ecclesiastes.
No. 13. The Song of Solomon.
No. 14. The Book of Isaiah.
No. 15. The Book of Jeremiah.
No. 16. The Book of Ezekiel.
No. 17. The Book of Daniel.
No. 18. The Book of Jonah.
No. 19. The Book of Malachi.
No. 20. The Gospel of Matthew.
No. 21. The Gospel of Luke.
No. 22. The Gospel of John.
No. 23. The Book of Acts.
No. 24. The two Epistles to Timothy.
No. 25. The Epistle to Philemon.
No. 26. The Epistle to the Hebrews.
No. 27. The Epistle of James.
No. 28. I John. II John. III John.
No. 29. The Epistle of Jude.
No. 30. The Book of Revelation.

Section VI
BIBLE TRIPLETS

In keeping score on the following, a correct answer after reading the first statement counts 4; after the second 3; after the third 2; after the fourth 1. (A score of 10 for the set of 3 is excellent.)

No. 1. THREE KINGDOMS

1

1. In the history of the chosen people, it followed the period of the judges.
2. Its second king remains today the great hero of his people.
3. The name of its third king has become synonymous with magnificence and wisdom.
4. Its end came not by conquest but through internal dissension.

2

1. It was what remained of the above kingdom, after the secession of the greater part of it.
2. Its capital city was Jerusalem.
3. Following a seventy year captivity, its people returned and re-established it.
4. Today, after centuries of oppression, it is still the hope of many that it may know a re-birth.

3

1. Its coming was foretold by John the Baptist.
2. Its founder made three remarkable statements about it: (a) it is not entered by loudly proclaimed allegiance.
3. (b) Little children are its ideal citizens.
4. (c) It is not militaristic—not of this world.

[Answers on page 97]

No. 2. THREE BIBLE LANDS

The status of all Bible lands has of course changed greatly during the centuries. The Nile valley is still Egypt but modern atlases do not show the empires of Babylonia and Chaldea. Persia has shrunk and become Iran; and Ethiopia, a dozen times mentioned in the Bible, is now Abyssinia. There are, however, three countries whose names have for us a far more modern sound and which the Bible mentions. (Their boundaries were of course not exactly the same then as now.) How many of the three can you identify?

1

1. It is mentioned but twice in the Bible, both times in the book of Romans.
2. From these references, it is evident that Paul hoped to preach the gospel there.
3. Whether he ever did so is uncertain. (Legend says he did.)
4. In our own time, this country has undergone a devastating civil war.

2

1. Immensely important as it was, its name is found in the Bible but three times—twice in the book of Acts.
2. The so-called revival of learning, following the "Dark Ages," had its rise there.
3. Many Jewish communities had become established there, long before the coming of Christianity.
4. It contained the capital city of the New Testament world.

3

1. At the dawn of Christianity, it had ceased to be a world power but its civilization covered all the western world.
2. In its language the books of our New Testament were written.
3. Paul preached one of his greatest sermons in its capital city.
4. We owe to it more than to any other country of ancient times, excepting only Palestine.

[Answers on page 97]

No. 3. THREE CITIES

1

1. Paul escaped Aretas, its governor, by being lowered from its walls in a basket.
2. Tradition declares it to be the oldest city still in existence.
3. It was once subject to David; and Benhadad, its king, was once captured by Ahab.
4. "Lawrence of Arabia" entered it at the head of his troops in the First World War.

2

1. It remained in alien hands long after Joshua's conquest, and was finally captured by David.
2. David made it his capital city and a capital city it remains today.
3. Outside its walls occurred the crucifixion.
4. Its capture was the great object of the Crusades.

3

1. Paul lived there for two years, "in his own hired house."
2. To the Christians living there he wrote one of his most important epistles.
3. Both Paul and Peter are said to have suffered martyrdom there.
4. In it is the largest church in the world.

No. 4. THREE LITTLE TOWNS

1

1. It was the boyhood home of King David.
2. Once, when it was garrisoned by the Philistines, three of his "mighty men" cut their way through to bring him water from its well.
3. In it is located the Church of the Nativity.
4. To it came Joseph and Mary, at a time when all the world was to be taxed.

[Answers on page 97]

2

1. In it Jesus "increased in wisdom and stature and in favor with God and man."
2. It was "a place of no history" (the Old Testament does not mention it) and of questionable reputation.
3. In its synagogue Jesus preached his first sermon.
4. One probably authentic site pointed out in it today is the so-called Virgin's Well.

3

1. It was the home of three warm, personal friends of Jesus.
2. Jesus was entertained at a feast there, in the home of Simon the Leper.
3. He is supposed to have spent there, in retirement, one day out of his last week.
4. The village lies about one and five-eighths miles from Jerusalem on the road to Jericho.

No. 5. THREE RIVERS

1

1. Though it is the most celebrated river of antiquity, it is not mentioned in the Bible by name.
2. Only within comparatively recent years has its source been discovered.
3. Its periodic rise and fall provided irrigation and fertility for one of the greatest of ancient peoples.
4. Upon its banks Joseph rose from slavery to a premiership.

2

1. Its mouth is below sea level.
2. Moses came to its banks but never crossed it.
3. In its waters John the Baptist baptized his converts.
4. Its name has come to be used as a synonym for death.

3

1. The Bible describes it but it is found on no map in any secular atlas.
2. Its source is named in the Scriptures.

[Answers on page 97]

3. A tree growing upon its banks is specifically described in the Bible.

4. He who tells of it says, "and I, John, saw these things."

No. 6. THREE MOUNTAINS

1

1. Though outside the confines of Palestine, the Hebrews regarded it as sacred.

2. Upon its slopes Moses was granted the vision of the burning bush.

3. From it he brought down the tablets of the law.

4. Standing in the entrance of one of its caves, Elijah heard "a still, small voice."

2

1. Though of comparatively slight elevation, it may perhaps claim to be the most famous mountain in the world.

2. The psalmist describes it as "beautiful for situation, the joy of the whole earth."

3. The whole Jewish people made it a place of pilgrimage.

4. Its name has come to be a synonym for that of the Christian Church.

3

1. Jesus passed over it on the day of his triumphant entrance into Jerusalem.

2. From its slopes he looked down upon Jerusalem and wept over it.

3. The Garden of Gethsemane is located upon it.

4. One of its four peaks, it has been claimed, is the Mount of Ascension.

No. 7. THREE ISLANDS

1

1. It lies in the Mediterranean, about equidistant from Europe, Asia and Africa.

2. Modern research has shown it to be the center of a very ancient civilization.

[Answers on page 98]

3. On the journey to Rome, Paul's ship touched there, at a port known as Fair Havens.

4. Paul's friend Titus, we learn from the epistle addressed to him, was at one time placed in charge of its churches.

2

1. It lies within sight of the Syrian coast and, during the "Bronze Age," was immensely valuable to man as a source of copper.

2. It was the birthplace of Barnabas.

3. Paul visited it upon his first missionary journey.

4. Its proconsul, Sergius Paulus, was an early convert to the Christian faith (Acts 13: 12).

3

1. It is the scene of one of the most dramatic shipwrecks recorded in classic literature.

2. After the wreck, Paul and his shipmates wintered there, " and the barbarous people showed us no little kindness " (Acts 28: 2).

3. The father of " the chief man of the island " was healed by Paul.

4. Its occupation and fortification by the British in modern times has been bitterly resented by Italy.

No. 8. THREE BIBLE STORIES

1

1. It is a fable, somewhat in the style of Æsop.

2. The " characters " are an olive tree, a fig tree, a grape vine, and a bramble.

3. The narrator, after telling it, had to flee for his life.

4. The man against whom it was directed met the fate predicted for him.

2

1. It was told by a prophet to a king, its purpose being to bring home to him a great sin.

[Answers on page 98]

2. A part of its poignant appeal lay in the fact that, as a boy, the king had tended sheep.
3. The story is climaxed in the words, "Thou art the man."
4. Its success was complete. The royal criminal was brought to his knees.

3

1. The scene shifts between a vineyard and a marketplace, the characters being the owner of a vineyard and successive groups of the unemployed.
2. The narrator of the story was Jesus; and its substance is a dispute over wages, between employer and employees.
3. Controversialists have often cited it as an argument for a living wage.
4. Rugged individualists, however, stress the familiar and thought-provoking words, "Is it not lawful for me to do what I will with mine own?"

No. 9. THREE PARABLE MEN

1

1. He was the father of two sons, both of whom in different ways caused him sorrow.
2. The parable in which he appears, takes its name from his younger son.
3. He is presented by Jesus as an illustration of the divine attitude toward both wayward and self-righteous men.
4. He is the true hero of what many regard as "the greatest short story in the world."

2

1. He was found wounded beside a stretch of notoriously dangerous road.
2. Two men, who from their occupations should have been first to help, saw him but "passed by on the other side."
3. Help was at last given him by a member of a despised and alien race.
4. The parable rightly takes its name from his rescuer.

3

1. The first sentence of the parable shows him setting forth upon a journey " into a far country."
2. Before departing, he intrusted to his servants considerable sums of money, " every one according to his several ability."
3. On his return he commended the servants who had wisely invested his money.
4. He strongly condemned a servant who had concealed his allotment and made no attempt to use it in any way.

No. 10.　THREE HEALINGS

1

1. Almost a dozen persons were healed at the same time.
2. Only one of them expressed any gratitude.
3. That one was a foreigner.
4. Jesus especially commended him.

2

1. The man healed was a beggar of Jericho.
2. The crowd reproved him for his loud calling.
3. The evil of which he wished to be cured was blindness.
4. His father's name was Timæus.

3

1. The subject of the healing was a boy, brought to Jesus by his father.
2. The healing is pictured in one of Raphael's greatest paintings.
3. It occurred just after Jesus had come down from the Mount of Transfiguration.
4. The disciples had attempted it and failed.

No. 11.　THREE SERMONS

1

1. It is beyond all question the most famous sermon ever preached.

[Answers on page 98]

2. It consists of about 100 Bible verses.

3. It takes its name not from its subject matter but from the place where it was preached.

4. It begins with the beatitudes and ends with the parable of the house founded upon a rock and that upon the sand.

2

1. It was preached upon a hill named for a god of Greek mythology.

2. Its text was an inscription upon a pagan altar.

3. It seems to have had no great immediate effect, though "some . . . believed."

4. The preacher was the apostle Paul.

3

1. It was preached in Jerusalem at a time when the city was crowded with "devout men from every nation under heaven."

2. The preacher was the same man who had thrice denied his master.

3. The text was taken from the prophet Joel.

4. It resulted in "about three thousand souls" being added to the local church.

No. 12. THREE ROMANCES

Identify, if you can, the principals in these love stories, recorded in the Bible.

1

1. A faithful servant was sent upon a long journey, to select a wife for his master's only son.

2. His choice was determined by what he believed to be a miraculous sign.

3. The two first met when the young man had gone out "to meditate in the field at eventide," and saw approaching the caravan that was bringing his bride.

4. The story climaxes in the words, "and she became his wife and he loved her."

[Answers on page 98]

2

1. The man was a wealthy citizen of Bethlehem.
2. The woman was a young Moabitish widow, whose devotion to her mother-in-law has become proverbial.
3. They became acquainted when she was a gleaner in his fields.
4. Their first-born son became the grandfather of King David.

3

1. (Hardest of the three.) It began in a squabble over water rights. Seven sisters, seeking to water their father's flocks, and driven off by rival shepherds, were aided by a young fugitive.
2. At home the sisters reported the matter and were bidden to return and invite the young man to be their guest.
3. Their father, who offered him a refuge and later gave him one of his daughters in marriage, is referred to as " a priest of Midian."
4. The young man returned as an ambassador of Jehovah to the court from which he had fled.

No. 13. THREE DREAMS

1

1. The ruler of the greatest empire of his time one night dreamed two dreams which puzzled him.
2. When the men whose task it was to interpret them failed him, his chief butler recalled a young prisoner who, two years before, had interpreted a dream for him.
3. Brought from the prison, the young man declared that the dreams foretold seven years of plenty, to be followed by seven years of famine.
4. The monarch rewarded him by putting him in charge of the plans to meet the impending crisis.

2

1. A soldier in a Midianitish army that was " like grasshoppers for multitude," had a dream that was both amusing and puzzling.

[Answers on pages 98–99]

2. He told it to a comrade who ventured to explain its meaning.
3. Two of the enemy, upon a scouting expedition, overheard their talk.
4. One of the eavesdroppers was the general of the opposing army.

3

1. The dreamer, Nebuchadnezzar, having dreamed the dream and been puzzled by it, could not recall it.
2. Notwithstanding, he threatened dire things against his "magicians, astrologers and soothsayers," if they did not both recall and interpret it.
3. This unreasonable demand was finally met by the prophet Daniel.
4. He explained the dream as a forecast of history.

No. 14. THREE BIBLE MOTHERS

1

1. Her husband was Elkanah, an Ephrathite, of Ramah.
2. Having no children, she vowed that, should she be given a son, she would dedicate him to the Lord.
3. While the boy was still quite young, she brought him to Eli, in Shiloh, where he served a priestly apprenticeship, his mother seeing him each year and bringing him "a little coat."
4. The boy came to be the last of the judges of his people.

2

1. The names of her two sons were Mahlon and Chilion.
2. Both took wives in the adjoining land of Moab.
3. Their death left their mother childless but not friendless.
4. She returned to her native village accompanied by her daughter-in-law.

3

1. (The hardest.) She was the mother of three children, two sons and a daughter, all prominent in the delivery of Israel from captivity.

[Answers on page 99]

2. Her more distinguished son (and probably the other also) was born under sentence of death.

3. The older son's first, abortive attempt to secure justice for his oppressed people led to his being driven into exile.

4. The name of the daughter was Miriam.

No. 15. THREE CHILDREN

1

1. He was born into a world where a sentence of death overhung all male children of his race.

2. When he could no longer be hidden at home, he was placed at the river's edge in a little ark made of papyrus and his older sister was put on guard.

3. There a king's daughter found and adopted him.

4. He grew up to be the great law-giver of his people.

2

1. We do not know her name but she is commonly identified by the name of her father, who is described as one of the rulers of the synagogue.

2. He came to Jesus saying that she was at the point of death and beseeching him to come and heal her.

3. On the way Jesus was delayed by another miracle of healing and

4. they were met by the news that the little girl was already dead.

5. Jesus' comment was, " Be not afraid, only believe." His words were fully justified.

3

1. He was a boy of Jesus' time, whose name we do not know; and we can identify him only by telling what food he carried on a certain day.

2. Andrew, Simon Peter's brother, brought him to Jesus as a forlorn hope, in time of need.

3. Jesus accepted what the boy had to offer.

4. His lunch took the place of " two hundred pennyworth of bread."

[Answers on page 99]

No. 16. THREE SONS

1

1. His early youth was spent with his father at Beersheba.
2. His father had other sons but of this one and his descendants great things had been prophesied.
3. Nevertheless his father felt himself moved to offer him as a sacrifice to Jehovah.
4. Divine revelation showed a better way.

2

1. The boy was the youngest of a large family of sons and his father's favorite.
2. The tragic disappearance of his next older brother (the father believed him to have been killed by a wild beast) had made him especially dear.
3. In time of famine, when the other brothers went down into Egypt leaving him at home, they were told that on their next visit they must bring him or they would get no more supplies.
4. His name has come to be synonymous with " favorite son."

3

1. A native of Lystra, we know the names of his mother and grandmother but not that of his father.
2. Two of the books of our New Testament are letters addressed to him.
3. He travelled widely with Paul and was of much help to him in his work.
4. While there was no blood kinship between them, Paul calls him " my beloved son."

No. 17. THREE KINGS

1

1. He was anointed years before he came to the throne.
2. Besides being a king, he was a musician and a poet.
3. To him is attributed the best loved poem ever written.
4. His life is more fully described than is that of any other king of Israel.

[Answers on page 99]

2

1. He was the last king to reign over the twelve tribes.
2. He built the first Jewish temple.
3. When asked to choose what gift he would have, he chose wisdom.
4. He was the son of the king described above.

3

1. A man of tremendous but ruthless energy, to whom the title of " the Great " has been applied.
2. He was visited by the " wise men from the east."
3. His fears, engendered by what they told him, occasioned the flight into Egypt.
4. He caused the slaying of his wife and children.

No. 18. THREE QUEENS

1

1. Her name is not given in the Bible but she may be identified by the name of the country over which she ruled. The New Testament refers to her as " the queen of the south."
2. Her people were great and wealthy traders, exporting gold, incense, spices and other costly goods.
3. The book of Kings relates that she visited King Solomon " to prove him with hard questions " and that, having seen his magnificence, she said, " the half was not told me."
4. Under the name of Balkis, she appears in both Christian and Mohammedan legends, one of which represents her as married to King Solomon. From this marriage the Abyssinian kings trace their descent.

2

1. The daughter of Ethbaal, king of Tyre, she became the wife of Ahab, king of Israel.
2. Brought up in the cult of Baal, she used her strong influence with her subservient husband to establish the same religion in Israel and, through her daughter Athaliah, in the neighboring kingdom of Judah.
3. This encouragement of Baal worship brought her into con-

[Answers on page 99]

flict with the prophet Elijah, who overthrew her priests in the famous encounter on Mount Carmel but himself fled when word was brought him that the queen sought his life.

4. Her name has become a synonym for an evil, vengeful woman.

3

1. An orphan in a strange land, her beauty was the occasion of her being made queen, by the king of the country which held her people in subjection.

2. Ignorant of her descent, an influential personal enemy of the relative in whose home she had been reared formed a plot, the purpose of which was the extermination of her race.

3. Guided by the wisdom of this kinsman, the young queen, acting with skill and courage, foiled the court intrigue and secured her people's triumph.

4. Her name is the title of one of the books of the Bible.

No. 19. THREE PRIESTS

1

1. He began his public career as spokesman for a greater brother, who felt himself not equal to this phase of leadership.

2. He accompanied the chosen people during the greater part of their wanderings in the wilderness.

3. During a prolonged absence of his brother, he was persuaded by the people to be their leader in an act of shameful apostasy.

4. He was succeeded by his son Eleazar, thus becoming the founder of an hereditary priesthood.

2

1. After the raising of Lazarus, he counselled his associates that it was better one (innocent) man should be put to death rather than that "the whole nation perish."

2. He held the office of high priest between A. D. 18 and 36 but only on sufferance of the Roman authorities.

3. He presided at the trial of Jesus, in "shameless disregard of the forms of law."

[Answers on pages 99–100]

4. In the courtyard of his palace, Peter thrice denied his Master.

3

1. (Hardest of the three.) In the book of Genesis, he is described as "the king of Salem . . . the priest of the most high God."

2. He is further represented to have blessed and entertained the patriarch Abraham, returning from the rescue of Lot and his household.

3. The writer of the Epistle to the Hebrews describes him as "without father, without mother, without descent, having neither beginning of days nor end of life."

4. Not only in Genesis and Hebrews but in the book of Psalms (a Psalm quoted by Jesus) is he mentioned with profound respect.

No. 20. THREE JUDGES

1

1. She was the fourth of the tribal leaders who succeeded Joshua—a judge and a prophetess.

2. To her was first applied the term "a mother in Israel."

3. So great was her prestige and influence that the commander in chief of her armies refused to go into battle unless she would accompany him.

4. The song called by her name is "one of the most ancient and magnificent remains of Hebrew literature."

2

1. While performing prodigies of strength, he never either ruled his own spirit or won any considerable following among his own people.

2. He believed that the secret of his great physical strength lay in his scrupulous observance of one of the vows taken by the Nazarites.

3. A woman's treachery delivered him into the hands of his enemies.

[Answers on page 100]

4. His story forms the subject of an opera by the French composer Camille Saint-Saëns.

3

1. His childhood was spent in the tabernacle, as a servant of the high priest.
2. Like the man who reared him, he lived to see his sons a disappointment and a disgrace to their calling.
3. Bitterly regretting the change from a theocracy to a monarchy, he yet bowed to the will of the people and anointed the king for whom they clamored.
4. It was to seek his counsel that King Saul visited the Witch of Endor.

No. 21. THREE STATESMEN

1

1. An extract from his memoirs reads, " I was in Shushan, the palace—for I was the king's cupbearer."
2. Learning of the deplorable situation of his homeland, he sought a leave of absence from the Persian court, that he might seek to remedy conditions there.
3. He was appointed governor (pechah) of the province of Judea and, under his leadership, the walls of Jerusalem were rebuilt.
4. A biblical authority says of him that he appears as " a gifted and accomplished man of action, well versed in the ways of the world and well equipped to meet difficult situations."

2

1. A cousin reared in his home came—largely through his influence—to be queen of Persia.
2. He had at court a personal enemy, who built a high gallows with the avowed purpose of hanging him thereon.
3. The irony of events forced this enemy to show him signal honor before the eyes of the whole city.
4. Through his influence an intended massacre of his people was averted and he was made " next unto King Ahasuerus—speaking peace to all his seed."

[Answers on page 100]

3

1. (The hardest.) A trusted friend of Israel's best loved king, he yet deserted him when his son rose in rebellion.
2. So astute were his counsels that it was said of him, "It was as if a man had inquired at the oracle of God."
3. Nevertheless a secret friend of the king's was able to overcome his influence.
4. Foreseeing the collapse of the insurrection, he set his affairs in order and took his own life.

No. 22. THREE CAPTAINS

1

1. As a young spy, he inspected the land into which he was later to lead a conquering army.
2. The minority report made, by himself and one other upon this expedition, was so bitterly resented that an attempt was made to lynch them.
3. He was the immediate successor of the great law-giver of his people.
4. His last years were saddened by his well grounded fears of the apostasy of his people.

2

1. A nephew of the king's he was, for the greater part of David's reign, the commander-in-chief of his armies.
2. A brave soldier and skillful leader, he was yet vindictive and at times ruthlessly cruel.
3. Utterly loyal to his king, he could deliberately disobey his orders, when they seemed to him unwise.
4. Though he "fled into the tabernacle of the Lord and caught hold on the horns of the altar," he was slain there at the order of King Solomon.

3

1. He describes himself as "a man under authority, having soldiers under me." (We do not know his name but he may be identified by the request which he made of Jesus.)

[Answers on page 100]

2. Jesus said of him, " I have not found so great faith—no, not in Israel."

3. Though a Roman, he was so sympathetic to the Jewish faith as to have built a synagogue for the local congregation.

4. Their elders deeply appreciated this and went to Jesus, seeking a favor on his behalf.

No. 23. THREE HEROES

1

1. When he destroyed an altar to Baal and, in place of it, erected one to Jehovah, he incurred the wrath of his fellow townsmen but he was saved by the shrewdness of his father.

2. At the beginning of a campaign in which he was vastly outnumbered by the enemy, he took the amazing course of reducing his army to a handful.

3. Scouting in the camp of the enemy, he was encouraged by hearing a soldier tell of a dream in which a loaf of bread knocked over a tent.

4. He led in a night attack three hundred of the most strangely armed men who ever won a victory.

2

1. He was one of a dozen men sent to spy out the land of Canaan and, in opposition to all his associates—save one, advised an immediate invasion.

2. This advice so infuriated the people that they wished to stone him.

3. He and one other were the only spies who survived to enter Canaan in the later, triumphant invasion.

4. He asked the privilege of subduing Hebron, which his fellow spies had said was inhabited by giants; and it was assigned to him as a reward for his fidelity.

3

1. Crown prince and a brave soldier, he is best known for having been one of the parties to a proverbial friendship.

2. He was once near to losing his life, as a result of having eaten a piece of honeycomb.

[Answers on page 100]

3. His father, who seemed to be subject to attacks of homicidal mania, once tried to slay him.

4. He was slain, together with his father and two brothers, in the battle of Mount Gilboa.

No. 24. THREE PRISONERS

1

1. At that time the recognized leader of the apostles, he was imprisoned for no better reason than a petty king's wish to gratify a powerful faction.
2. Effectually to prevent his escape, he was guarded by four quaternions of soldiers, between two of whom he slept, bound by two chains.
3. The circumstances of his deliverance were such that he himself did not believe it " but thought he saw a vision."
4. Friends praying for his release were so much surprised by the prompt answer to their prayers that they questioned the sanity of the maid who reported it.

2

1. His longest imprisonment was begun when the authorities rescued him from a mob.
2. The conditions of his imprisonment were made less harsh by the fact of his Roman citizenship.
3. The Bible narrative leaves him still in custody but it is believed that he was later released and continued his ministry.
4. He is the most famous of all New Testament prisoners.

3

1. He was a companion of the above on his missionary journey into Macedonia.
2. In Philippi, after being first beaten, they were placed in the inner prison, their feet made fast in the stocks.
3. Their midnight songs of praise were interrupted by " a mighty earthquake."
4. Their deliverance was accompanied by the conversion of their jailor and a public apology from the authorities.

[Answers on page 100]

No. 25. THREE PATRIARCHS

1

1. One of the first great pioneers of history, he set out at the age of seventy-five, taking with him all his possessions, to establish himself in a land he had never seen.
2. In his new home he prospered and lived amicably with neighbors whose ways he nevertheless disapproved.
3. It was foretold of him that his descendants would one day inherit the land in which he himself was a sojourner.
4. He has been called the Father of the Faithful.

2

1. He is introduced to us as a prosperous citizen of the land of Uz, "perfect and upright, one that feared God and eschewed evil."
2. The drama in which his story is told contains some of the sublimest and most beautiful passages of all Scripture.
3. As a trial of his faith, he was visited with an almost unparalleled series of calamities.
4. His character survived the ordeal and the story has a happy ending.

3

1. He is described as "just and devout, waiting for the consolation of Israel."
2. Patient in his attendance upon the temple, he was at last rewarded by the sight for which he had long waited.
3. He described the Christ Child (brought to the temple after the custom of the law) as "a light to lighten the Gentiles and the glory of thy people Israel."
4. He blessed Joseph and Mary but warned Mary of a sword that should pierce through her own soul.

[Answers on page 100]

ANSWERS

Section VI
BIBLE TRIPLETS

No. 1. THREE KINGDOMS
1. The kingdom of (undivided) Israel.
2. The kingdom of Judah.
3. The Kingdom of God (or Heaven).

No. 2. THREE BIBLE LANDS
1. Spain (Rom. 15: 24, 28).
2. Italy (Acts 18: 2; 27: 1).
3. Greece (Acts 20: 2).

No. 3. THREE CITIES
1. Damascus.
2. Jerusalem.
3. Rome.

No. 4. THREE LITTLE TOWNS
1. Bethlehem.
2. Nazareth.
3. Bethany.

No. 5. THREE RIVERS
1. The Nile.
2. The Jordan.
3. The River of the Water of Life (Rev. 22: 1).

No. 6. THREE MOUNTAINS

1. Mount Sinai (called also Mount Horeb).
2. Mount Zion.
3. Mount of Olives.

No. 7. THREE ISLANDS

1. Crete (Candia).
2. Cyprus.
3. Malta (Melita).

No. 8. THREE BIBLE STORIES

1. Judges 9: 7–21.
2. II Sam. 12: 1–15.
3. Matt. 20: 1–16.

No. 9. THREE PARABLE MEN

1. The father of The Prodigal Son.
2. The man helped by The Good Samaritan.
3. The business man who allotted The Talents.

No. 10. THREE HEALINGS

1. The cleansing of the ten lepers (Luke 17: 12–19).
2. Blind Bartimæus (Mark 10: 46–52).
3. The healing of the demoniac boy (Mark 9: 17–29).

No. 11. THREE SERMONS

1. The Sermon on the Mount.
2. Paul's sermon on Mars Hill.
3. Peter's sermon on the day of Pentecost.

No. 12. THREE ROMANCES

1. Isaac and Rebekah.
2. Ruth and Boaz.
3. Moses and Zipporah.

No. 13. THREE DREAMS

1. Seven fat and seven lean kine; seven good and seven blasted ears of corn.
2. A cake of barley bread which fell in the camp and overturned a tent.
3. A towering figure, with feet " partly of clay," overthrown by a stone " cut out without hands," which later grew until " it became a great mountain and filled the whole earth."

No. 14. THREE BIBLE MOTHERS

1. Hannah (I Sam. 1: 1–2).
2. Naomi (Ruth 1: 2).
3. Jochebed (Ex. 6: 20; Num. 26: 59).

No. 15. THREE CHILDREN

1. Moses.
2. Jairus's daughter.
3. The boy with the " five barley loaves and two small fishes."

No. 16. THREE SONS

1. Isaac—son of Abraham.
2. Benjamin—son of Jacob.
3. Timothy—" son " of Paul.

No. 17. THREE KINGS

1. David (few will question that " the best loved poem " is the 23rd Psalm).
2. Solomon.
3. Herod the Great.

No. 18. THREE QUEENS

1. The Queen of Sheba.
2. Jezebel.
3. Esther.

No. 19. THREE PRIESTS
1. Aaron.
2. Caiaphas.
3. Melchizedek (Gen. 14: 18).

No. 20. THREE JUDGES
1. Deborah.
2. Sampson.
3. Samuel.

No. 21. THREE STATESMEN
1. Nehemiah.
2. Mordecai.
3. Ahithophel.

No. 22. THREE CAPTAINS
1. Joshua.
2. Joab.
3. The Centurion who sought from Jesus the healing of a faithful servant.

No. 23. THREE HEROES
1. Gideon.
2. Caleb.
3. Jonathan.

No. 24. THREE PRISONERS
1. Peter (Acts 12).
2. Paul.
3. Silas (Acts 16).

No. 25. THREE PATRIARCHS
1. Abraham.
2. Job.
3. Simeon.

Section VII
THE BIBLE AND THE POETS

> Within that awful volume lies
> The mystery of mysteries!
> Happiest they of human race,
> To whom God has given grace
> To read, to fear, to hope, to pray,
> To lift the latch and force the way;
> And better had they ne'er been born
> Who read to doubt, or read to scorn.
> —Sir Walter Scott.

No one can really know English literature without knowing the Bible and nowhere is this more evident than in the reading of the poets. Beginning with the first author named in the latest edition of Bartlett's *Familiar Quotations* (Cædmon, "the father of English song") there has not been one generation of poets (Not one poet?) that has not drawn liberally upon the Bible for illustration and imagery.

Among the countless quotations that might be cited, the following will serve as illustrations. If one wishes to keep score, each correct answer may count 20: 100 for each set of questions, 1,500 for the series.

No. 1. THE BIBLE AND SHAKESPEARE

Many times this number of quotations could easily be given.

1. In "Richard III," a hired assassin cries:

    > How fain, like Pilate, would I wash my hands
    > Of this most grievous, guilty murder done.

Explain the reference.

[Answers on page 115]

2. In "Henry VIII," we find the lines:

> Saba was never
> More covetous of wisdom and fair virtue
> Than this pure soul. . . .

What biblical incident is referred to?

3. A character in "Henry VI," Part I, exclaims:

> Stay, stay thy hand! thou art an Amazon
> And fightest with the sword of Deborah.

Who was Deborah?

4. In "Henry VI," Part III, we read:

> To keep that oath were more impiety
> Than Jephtha's, when he sacrificed his daughter.

What oath had Jephtha taken?

5. In "The Merry Wives of Windsor," Sir John Falstaff says:

> I fear no Goliath with a weaver's beam.

Why a weaver's beam?

No. 2. THE BIBLE AND TENNYSON

A handful out of many possible quotations.

1. In "The Last Tournament" occurs the line:

> For I have flung these pearls and found thee swine.

The reference is to what saying of Jesus?

2. In "The Princess," is mentioned:

> A Jonah's gourd,
> Up in one night and due to sudden sun.

Explain the allusion.

[Answers on page 115]

3. Explain the words from "Locksley Hall":

> Joshua's moon in Ajalon.

4. What is meant by the following words from "Becket"?

> A whole Peter's sheet.

5. (A really hard one.) One of the speakers in "A Dream of Fair Women" says:

> Moreover it is written that my race
>   Hew'd Ammon hip and thigh, from Aroer
> On Arnon unto Minneth.

Who is speaking?

No. 3. THE BIBLE AND WHITTIER

Bible references are numerous throughout Whittier's's poems.

1. "Ichabod" is the title given a poem in which he voiced his bitter disappointment in Daniel Webster. Why this title?

2. In a poem often sung as a hymn, Whittier wrote:

> The healing of his seamless dress
> Is by our beds of pain.

How do we know that Jesus wore a seamless garment?

3. What miracle is referred to in the lines immediately following?

> We touch him in life's throng and press,
> And we are whole again.

4. What authority was there for writing, in the dedication to the "Songs of Labor":

> He whose name we breathe with awe
> The coarse mechanic vesture wore.

[Answers on pages 115–116]

5. What incident is referred to in the lines:

> By him who gave the tangled ram
> To spare the child of Abraham.

No. 4. THE BIBLE AND THE POETS (I)

1. In "Two Men," Edwin Arlington Robinson writes:

> Melchizedek he praised the Lord
> And gave some wine to Abraham;
> And who can tell what else he did
> Must be more learned than I am.

Can *you* tell anything more about Melchizedek?

2. In the poem "Rimmon," Rudyard Kipling writes:

> Duly with knees that fain to quake—
> Bent head and shaded brow—
> Yet once again, for my fathers' sake,
> In Rimmon's House I bow.

What Old Testament character bowed in the House of Rimmon?

3. What incident in the life of the apostle Peter is suggested in the following lines by Elizabeth Barrett Browning? ("A View Across the Roman Campagna.")

> Peter, Peter! He does not speak,
> He is not as rash as in old Galilee.
> Safer a ship, though it toss and leak,
> Than a reeling foot on a rolling sea.

4. What victory is celebrated in the lines of Thomas Moore:

> Sound the loud timbrel o'er Egypt's dark sea!
> Jehovah has triumphed, his people are free!
> Sing, for the pride of the tyrant is broken,
> His chariot, his horsemen all splendid and brave . . .

[Answers on page 116]

5. John Hay, in his poem "Religion and Doctrine," has:

> I know not what this man may be,
> Sinner or Saint, but, as for me,
> One thing I know, that I am he,
> Who once was blind, and now I see.

What story is paraphrased?

No. 5. THE BIBLE AND THE POETS (II)

1. Of what tower would Laurence Housman remind us, when he writes:

> Nation by nation still goes unforgiven
> Building high towers which will not reach to heaven.

2. Clarify the lines of George Wither:

> They're Judas' kisses now,
> Since that they proved untrue.

3. In a quatrain, entitled "The Bee and the Blossom," Father Tabb asks:

> Why stand ye idle, blossoms bright,
> The livelong Summer day.

From what parable of Jesus is he quoting?

4. One of Kipling's poems begins:

> Jack Barrett went to Quetta
> Because they told him to

and ends by saying (in effect) that on the day of judgment

> I should not like to be the man
> Who sent Jack Barrett there.

What incident of Bible history gives the poem its title, "The Story of Uriah"?

[Answers on page 116]

5. Who is referred to in the following lines from Longfellow's sonnet on "St. John's, Cambridge"?

> Then I remembered one of whom was said,
> In the world's darkest hour, "Behold thy son."

No. 6. THE BIBLE AND THE POETS (III)

1. What event is referred to in the following stanzas, from J. G. Holland's poem, "Gradatim"?

> Only in dreams is a ladder thrown
> From the weary earth to the sapphire walls;
> But the dream departs and the vision falls;
> And the sleeper wakes on his pillow of stone.

2. Charles Mackay's poem on "Tubal Cain" begins:

> Old Tubal Cain was a man of might,
> In the days when the earth was young.

Tell more about Tubal Cain.

3. In Rudyard Kipling's "The Rhyme of the Three Sealers," we read:

> A dog-toothed laugh laughed Reuben Paine, and bared his flenching knife,
> "Yea, skin for skin, and all that he hath a man will give for his life."

The second line is a direct quotation from whom?

4. "Stilling the Tempest," a quatrain by Father Tabb, ends with the lines:

> The torrent of her tresses she did spill
> Before his feet; and lo, the troubled wave
> Of passion heard his whisper, "Peace, be still."

What two biblical incidents are referred to?

106 [Answers on pages 116–117]

5. Isaac Watts, in the hymn "There Is a Land of Pure Delight," says:

> Could we but stand where Moses stood
> And view the landscape o'er . . .

Where did Moses stand?

No. 7. THE BIBLE AND THE POETS (IV)

1. What passage of Scripture is suggested by the first line of Henry F. Lyte's hymn:

> Abide with me, fast falls the eventide . . . ?

2. Which one of Jesus' parables is referred to in the following lines by Richard Crashaw?

> Two went to pray? Or rather say,
> One went to brag, the other to pray.

3. The second stanza of Reginald Heber's hymn, "The Son of God Goes Forth to War," begins:

> That martyr first, whose eagle eye
> Could pierce beyond the grave,
> He saw his master in the sky . . .

Name the martyr referred to.

4. In "Aurora Leigh," Elizabeth Barrett Browning has written:

> Earth's crammed with heaven
> And every common bush afire with God,
> But only he who sees takes off his shoes. . . .

To what biblical incident does she refer?

5. The eight times repeated tag line of Rudyard Kipling's rather terrible poem, "Boots," is:

> There's no discharge in that war.

Do you find in it any echo of Scripture?

[Answers on page 117]

No. 8. THE BIBLE AND THE POETS (V)

1. In a poem called "The Little Cloud," John Howard Bryant wrote:

> As when, on Carmel's sterile steep,
>   The ancient prophet bowed the knee
> And seven times sent his servant forth
>   To look toward the sea. . . .

Who was "the ancient prophet"?

2. In Kipling's "Piet," we have the lines:

> "I've 'eard 'im callin' from the ground
>   Like Abel's blood of old."

Explain the allusion.

3. Father Tabb, in a quatrain on "Milton," wrote:

> A flaming sword before thine eyes
> Had shut thee out from Paradise.

What biblical incident is referred to?

4. William Blake has written:

> Jesus was sitting in Moses' chair,
> They brought the trembling woman there,
> Moses commands she be stoned to death,
> What was the sound of Jesus' breath?

What incident in the life of the Master is referred to?

5. John Milton, in "Paradise Lost," has:

> . . . birds in orderly array on wing
> Come summoned over Eden to receive
> Their names of thee. . . .

By whom were they named?

[Answers on page 117]

No. 9. THE BIBLE AND THE POETS (VI)

1. In Sam Walter Foss's poem, "The House by the Side of the Road," occur the lines:

> I would not sit in the scorner's seat
> Or hurl the cynic's ban . . .

What echo of the Psalms do you find here?

2. In "Paradise Lost," John Milton refers to:

> . . . that uxorious king whose heart, though large,
> Beguiled by fair idolatresses, fell
> To idols foul.

What king is meant?

3. James Russell Lowell, in "The Present Crisis," wrote:

> . . . where today the martyr stands
> On the morrow crouches Judas with the silver in his hands.

What is the incident referred to?

4. A sonnet by Father Tabb begins:

> I wrestled, as did Jacob, till the dawn
> With the reluctant spirit of the night. . . .

What is the incident?

5. In "One Woman," a sonnet by Zoë Akins, we read:

> . . . went her way with tireless feet,
> When night had passed and the long day begun;—
> So Hagar faced the desert with her son.

Explain the allusion.

No. 10. THE BIBLE AND THE POETS (VII)

1. One of the most beautiful of biblical paraphrases is Joseph Addison's hymn beginning

[Answers on pages 117–118]

> The spacious firmament on high . . .

How does the Bible passage itself begin?

2. From Father Tabb's "The Song of the Man":

> She plucked and ate, and I did eat,
> And lost alike are we. . . .

What is the reference?

3. George Herbert's lines:

> Teach me, my God and King,
> In all things thee to see,
> And what I do in anything,
> To do it as for thee,

paraphrase one of Paul's injunctions. What is it?

4. John Keats, in his "Ode to a Nightingale," describes Ruth as standing, "sick for home . . . amid the alien corn." For what land was she homesick?

5. Emerson, in "The Problem," writes:

> Ever the fiery Pentecost
> Girds with one flame the countless host.

To what is he referring?

No. 11. THE BIBLE AND THE POETS (VIII)

1. John Milton, in the opening lines of "Paradise Lost," speaks of:

> That shepherd who first taught the chosen seed
> In the beginning how the heavens and earth
> Rose out of Chaos.

What was the shepherd's name?

[Answers on page 118]

2. When Rudyard Kipling, in his "Recessional," wrote:

> Still stands thine ancient sacrifice,
> An humble and a contrite heart,

from which book of the Bible was he quoting?

3. In "A Ballad of Trees and the Master," Sidney Lanier has:

> When Death and Shame would woo Him last,
> From under the trees they drew Him last.

Where did these trees grow?

4. "Tears," a famous sonnet by Lizette Woodworth Reese, closes with the words:

> . . . each hath what once he stayed to weep,
> Homer his sight, David his little lad.

Who was the "little lad"?

5. (The hardest.) Robert Burns' "The Cottar's Saturday Night," Stanza XIV, begins:

> The priest-like father reads the sacred page,
>   How Abram was the friend of God on high;
> How Moses bade eternal warfare wage
>   With Amalek's ungracious progeny.

Why is "Amalek's progeny" termed "ungracious"?

No. 12. THE BIBLE AND THE POETS (IX)

1. In the famous line, "The conscious water saw its God and blushed," Richard Crashaw refers to what biblical incident?

2. When, in Edgar Allan Poe's "Raven," the cry is uttered: "Is there—*is* there balm in Gilead?—tell me—tell me I implore," what biblical writer is quoted?

[Answers on page 118]

3. In a poem beginning:

> The Assyrian came down like the wolf on the fold
> And his cohorts were gleaming with purple and gold,

Lord Byron describes what episode in Jewish history?

4. Ralph Waldo Emerson closes his poem " Good-bye " with the words:

> For what are they all in their high conceit,
> When man in the bush with God may meet.

What incident is referred to?

5. Rudyard Kipling, in " Pharaoh and the Sergeant," writes:

> Said England unto Pharaoh, " You've had miracles before,
> When Aaron turned your rivers into blood."

Explain the reference.

No. 13. THE BIBLE AND THE POETS (X)

1. William Cowper, in one of his poems, writes:

> Who gives the lilies clothing
> Will clothe his people too.

What passage of Scripture does he paraphrase?

2. In Matthew Arnold's sonnet, " East London," we read:

> I met a preacher there I knew and said,
> " Ill and o'erworked, how fare you on this scene? "
> " Bravely," he said, " for I of late have been
> Much cheered with thoughts of Christ, *the living bread.*"

By whom and to whom was Christ thus described?

3. In one of his lyrics, Father Tabb writes of Christopher Columbus:

[Answers on pages 118–119]

> God sent thee from the crowded ark,
> Christ-bearer, like the dove. . . .

Explain the allusion.

4. George Matheson, Edinburgh's famous blind preacher, wrote a hymn in which occurs the line:

> Rend each man's temple veil and bid it fall.

Explain the allusion.

5. Amplify the lines of John Milton, in "Samson Agonistes":

> Eyeless in Gaza, at the mill of slaves,
> Himself in bonds, under Philistian yoke!

No. 14. THE BIBLE AND THE POETS (XI)

In the case of this quiz and that which follows, we think of the authors primarily as hymn writers, not poets, though it is of course impossible to draw a line between them.

Many hymns are simply Scriptural paraphrases, while others are seen to have been suggested by some Bible verse or incident.

Name the biblical inspiration of as many of the following as you can.

1. Hushed Was the Evening Hymn (James D. Burns).
2. Angels from the Realms of Glory (James Montgomery).
3. I think When I Read that Sweet Story of Old (Jemima Luke).
4. Fierce Was the Wild Billow (Anatolius, 8th Century. Translated by John M. Neale).
5. Hark! The Voice of Jesus Calling (Daniel Marsh).

No. 15. THE BIBLE AND THE POETS (XII)

Name the biblical inspiration of as many of the following hymns as you can.

1. Master, No Offering Costly and Sweet (Edwin P. Parker).

[Answers on page 119]

2. Ride on in Majesty (Rev. H. H. Milman).
3. Break Thou the Bread of Life (Mary A. Lathbury).
4. There is a Green Hill Far Away (Cecil F. Alexander).
5. Come, Ye Faithful, Raise the Strain (John of Damascus, about 750. Translated by John M. Neale).

ANSWERS

Section VII
THE BIBLE AND THE POETS

No. 1. THE BIBLE AND SHAKESPEARE

1. Pilate publicly washed his hands, as a symbol of his (professed) innocence of the death of Jesus (Matt. 27: 24).
2. The visit of the Queen of Sheba to Solomon (I Kings 10: 1–2).
3. A woman judge of Israel. It would appear (Shakespeare to the contrary notwithstanding) that Deborah herself did no fighting (Judges 4: 4–9).
4. That, in the event of victory, he would sacrifice to the Lord the first living thing that met him on his return from battle (Judges 11: 30–40).
5. It was said of Goliath that "the staff of his spear was like a weaver's beam" (I Sam. 17: 7).

No. 2. THE BIBLE AND TENNYSON

1. Neither cast ye your pearls before swine (Matt. 7: 6).
2. The Lord caused a gourd to grow up for a shade over Jonah's head, while he waited for the destruction of Nineveh (Jonah 4: 6).
3. Joshua had commanded the moon (and the sun) to stand still, that a battle might be continued (Joshua 10).
4. The reference is to Peter's vision at the home of Simon the tanner, in Joppa (Acts 10: 11).
5. Jephtha's daughter (Judges 11).

No. 3. THE BIBLE AND WHITTIER

1. And she named the child Ichabod, saying, "The glory is departed" (I Sam. 4: 21).
2. It is mentioned as part of the raiment for which the soldiers detailed to the crucifixion cast lots (John 19: 23).
3. The healing of the woman who touched Jesus' garment on his way to the raising of Jairus's daughter (Luke 8: 44).
4. The common report of Jesus' time (Mark 6: 3).
5. Abraham's sacrifice of Isaac (Gen. 22: 13).

No. 4. THE BIBLE AND THE POETS (I)

1. From Genesis 14: 18, we learn that he was "king of Salem . . . the priest of the most high God."
2. Naaman, the Syrian (II Kings 5: 18).
3. His seeking to walk upon the water, to meet the Master (Matt. 14: 29).
4. The overwhelming of the hosts of Pharaoh in the Red Sea (Ex. 15: 20).
5. The healing of the man born blind (John 9).

No. 5. THE BIBLE AND THE POETS (II)

1. The Tower of Babel (Gen. 11: 4).
2. A kiss was the sign by which Judas betrayed the Master (Matt. 26: 48).
3. The Parable of the Laborers in the Vineyard (Matt. 20: 6).
4. David's taking of Bathsheba, the wife of Uriah the Hittite (II Sam. 11: 15).
5. The Apostle John (John 19: 26–27).

No. 6. THE BIBLE AND THE POETS (III)

1. Jacob's vision at Bethel (Gen. 28: 11–22).
2. He was "an instructor of every artificer in brass and iron" (Gen. 4: 22).
3. From Satan: as might be expected, the words are untrue (Job 2: 4).

4. The bringing of the alabaster box of ointment to Jesus by the woman "which was a sinner" (Luke 7: 37-38). Jesus stilling the storm upon the lake of Galilee (Matt. 8: 24-26).

5. Upon Mount Nebo also called Mount Pisgah (Deut. 34: 1).

No. 7. THE BIBLE AND THE POETS (IV)

1. That describing the meeting of the risen Christ with the two disciples upon the road to Emmaus (Luke 24).

2. The parable of The Pharisee and the Publican (Luke 18: 10-14).

3. Stephen (Acts 7: 56).

4. That of Moses and the burning bush (Ex. 3).

5. It is a direct quotation from Ecclesiastes 8: 8.

No. 8. THE BIBLE AND THE POETS (V)

1. Elijah (I Kings 18: 42-44).

2. "... and the Lord said unto Cain ... thy brother's blood crieth unto me from the ground" (Gen. 4: 9-10).

3. The reference is to the flaming sword which barred Adam and Eve out of the Eden from which they had been banished (Gen. 3: 24).

4. That of the woman taken in adultery and brought to Jesus (John 8: 3-11).

5. By Adam (Gen. 2: 19-20).

No. 9. THE BIBLE AND THE POETS (VI)

1. "Blessed is the man that walketh not in the counsel of the ungodly ... nor sitteth in the seat of the scornful" (Psalm 1: 1).

2. Solomon (I Kings 11: 1-3).

3. That of Judas, returning to the chief priests the thirty pieces of silver paid him for the betrayal of Jesus (Matt. 27).

4. At Peniel, on his return to his native land and a justly angry brother, Jacob wrestled all night alone and won the blessing of his adversary (Gen. 32: 24-32).

5. The expulsion of Hagar by Abraham (Gen. 21).

No. 10. THE BIBLE AND THE POETS (VII)

1. The heavens declare the glory of God and the firmament showeth his handiwork (Pslam 19).
2. To the fruit of the tree of the knowledge of good and evil (Gen. 3).
3. "Whether therefore ye eat, or drink, or whatsoever ye do, do all to the glory of God" (I Cor. 10: 31).
4. Moab, the land of her birth.
5. The phenomena attending the day of Pentecost (Acts 2: 3).

No. 11. THE BIBLE AND THE POETS (VIII)

1. Moses. "Now Moses kept the flocks of Jethro, his father-in-law" (Ex. 3: 1).
2. "The sacrifices of God are a broken spirit: a broken and a contrite heart, O God, thou wilt not despise" (Psalm 51: 17).
3. In the Garden of Gethsemane (John 18: 1; Matt. 26: 36).
4. Absalom (II Sam. 18: 33).
5. Amalek had attacked the Israelites at a time when they were ill prepared to defend themselves (Deut. 25: 17). Thus, though Amalek was defeated, the resentment of Israel against him was keen (Ex. 17: 13–16).

No. 12. THE BIBLE AND THE POETS (IX)

1. The turning of water into wine, at Cana of Galilee (John 2: 1–11).
2. Jeremiah 8: 22.
3. The destruction of Sennacherib (Also the title of the poem) (II Kings 19: 35).
4. Moses and the burning bush (Ex. 3: 2).
5. The reference is of course to the plagues of Egypt (Ex. 7 and 8).

No. 13. THE BIBLE AND THE POETS (X)

1. "Consider the lilies of the field how they grow. . . . Shall not he much more clothe you?" (Matt. 6: 28–30).

2. By Jesus himself, to a group of Jews who "murmured" (John 6: 41–51).

3. Noah sent forth a dove from the stranded ark, to learn whether or not the waters of the flood had abated (Gen. 8: 8).

4. On the day of the crucifixion (Matt. 27: 51), the veil which shut the most sacred part of the temple from the rest of the enclosure (Ex. 40: 3; Lev. 16: 2) "was rent in twain, from the top to the bottom."

5. After Samson's betrayal by Delilah, the Philistines put out his eyes and "he did grind in the prison house" (Judges 16: 21).

No. 14. THE BIBLE AND THE POETS (XI)

1. The Call of Samuel (I Sam. 3).
2. The Song of the Angels to the Shepherds (Luke 2).
3. Jesus Blessing the Children (Mark 10: 13).
4. Jesus Stilling the Tempest (Mark 4: 35–41).
5. John 4: 35.

No. 15. THE BIBLE AND THE POETS (XII)

1. The gift of Mary Magdalen (John 12: 3).
2. The Triumphal Entry (Matt. 21: 6–11).
3. The Feeding of the Five Thousand (Mark 6: 41).
4. The Crucifixion.
5. The Resurrection.

Section VIII
MISCELLANEOUS QUIZZES

No. 1. WHAT THE BIBLE SAYS ABOUT MONEY

"Jesus had far more to say about money," some one has told us, " than he has to say about heaven "; and, when we study his teachings, we find this is quite true. Not that he regards money as, in itself, of much importance, but, as one theologian has put it, " it was a straw which showed which way the wind blew." Also, it was something dangerous to handle—like dynamite.

The following questions, suggested by verses in the gospels and in the epistles are on what might be called Bible economics.

1. What did Jesus say implying that money is dangerous?
2. Which one of the parables seems to teach that money (and other things) should be used—not put in cold storage?
3. Did Jesus ever say anything suggesting caution in giving away money—and other things?
4. In the parable of the Rich Fool, what was wrong with the man anyway?
5. What incident in Jesus' life seems to show that he valued a gift of love more than almsgiving?
6. What did Jesus say about the manner of giving money?
7. What parable seems to show that men should be paid " not according to their services but according to their needs " ?
8. What did Paul say about regularity and system in giving?
9. What did he say about the spirit of giving?
10. What did he say about the love of money?

No. 2. WHAT THE BIBLE SAYS ABOUT WISDOM

A great English poet said of wisdom that it is rare in youth and beauty; one of his successors said, " Wisdom is ofttimes nearer when we stoop than when we soar "; and a third great

[Answers on page 137]

English poet said, "Knowledge comes but wisdom lingers." The best things said about wisdom, however, are to be found in the Bible and especially in the books of Proverbs and Ecclesiastes.
1. What is the beginning of wisdom?
2. Where may the voice of wisdom be heard?
3. What is the price of wisdom?
4. What are its rewards?
5. What are some of its uses?
6. What effect has it upon personal appearance?
7. How does wisdom compare with folly?
8. What of the power of wisdom as compared with money?
9. As compared with a strong army and navy?
10. What is the most favorable time for seeking wisdom?

No. 3. WHAT THE BIBLE TELLS US ABOUT LOVE

How well do you know the Bible? Not as literature, history, or even theology, but as a book of personal helpfulness, of moral and religious first aid? The following is only a guessing game but some of the questions will bear much brooding over.

Perhaps there is no more important word in the whole Bible than "love." The whole of the New Testament is devoted to the purpose of showing that God is love. God's affectionate devotion to mankind in the face of man's many errors runs through the Old Testament.

1. On the basis of what New Testament chapter did Henry Drummond call love "the greatest thing in the world"?
2. What is the most remarkable thing said about love in this chapter?
3. What is the relation of love to "the law"?
4. What is the relation of love to fear?
5. Is love of God commanded in the Old Testament as well as in the New?
6. What has the Old Testament to say about loving one's neighbor?
7. Can one love God and hate his fellow men?
8. What reason does John give for loving God?
9. Jesus gave his followers a reason for loving their enemies. What was it?

[Answers on pages 137–138]

10. What was the measure of love that Jesus wished his disciples to have for one another?

No. 4. BIBLE OCCUPATIONS

The life of Bible times, especially that of the Old Testament, was of course much simpler than that of our day but it would be easy to list a score of Bible trades and callings: shipbuilders, lawyers, merchants, weavers, dyers, potters, bakers, even confectioners and jewelers. Can you name the occupations followed by the men whose names are given below? (Some of them are hard.)

1. Jabal.
2. Jubal.
3. Tubal-cain.
4. Nimrod.
5. Amos. (He is of course known to us as a prophet, but he explains that he followed a humbler occupation.)
6. Peter and Andrew.
7. Lazarus. (The Lazarus of Jesus' parable; not the brother of Mary and Martha.)
8. Zacchæus.
9. Demetrius, of Ephesus.
10. Simon—with whom Simon Peter lodged, while in Joppa.
11. Cornelius, of Cæsarea.
12. Paul. (He was of course an apostle but he also had a trade by which at times he earned his living.)
13. Alexander, of whom Paul wrote that "he did me much harm."

No. 5. BIBLE LETTERS

Of the 27 books which make up our New Testament, 21 are letters. Can you divide them under the following heads:

1. Nine are addressed to groups of Christians in various cities or provinces.
2. Seven are known by the names of their writers.
3. Four are known by the names of their (individual) addressees.

[Answers on pages 138–139]

4. One is addressed to a whole people.
5. The Revelation, while commonly not classified as a letter, might be so considered. Why?

No. 6. BIBLE WILD ANIMALS

1. Insisting that he was quite able to go out and fight the Philistine champion, Goliath, the boy David explained that his father's sheep had been attacked by two wild animals, both of which he had killed. What animals were they?
2. Speaking of his own homelessness, Jesus said that certain animals had holes, while he himself had not where to lay his head. What animals did he name?
3. "Can the . . . change his spots?" is the most familiar passage in which the name of this animal is mentioned.
4. In Jesus' picture of himself as The Good Shepherd, he describes this animal as preying upon the sheep.

No. 7. BIRDS OF THE BIBLE

1. An Old Testament story describes them as bringing food, twice a day, to a prophet.
2. In one of the most moving verses of "the Jewish Hymn Book," the psalmist envies this bird its wings. "For then would I fly away and be at rest."
3. A migratory bird, of which the psalmist says that it has found in God's altars a nest for herself, where she may lay her young.
4. The commonest of our domestic fowls, it is mentioned by Jesus in a comparison of surpassing beauty and tenderness.

No. 8. BIBLE INSECTS

The names of the following insects (and certain others, depending upon the translation used) are found in the Bible. Can you name one connection in which each is mentioned: 1. Bees. 2. Locusts. 3. Flies. 4. Grasshoppers. 5. Ants.

[Answers on pages 139–140]

No. 9. BIBLE WEAPONS

The weapons mentioned in the Bible are of course those of all ancient peoples. The apostle Paul, however, in a famous figurative passage, gave each of the following its spiritual equivalent. Can you name them?
1. The breastplate of . . .
2. The shield of . . .
3. The helmet of . . .
4. The sword of . . .

No. 10. BIBLE MUSICAL INSTRUMENTS

1. What instrument was played to soothe the maniacal moods of a king, by a youth who later succeeded him upon the throne?
2. What martial instrument was used by a small band of men in a night attack upon an enemy by whom they were greatly outnumbered?
3. The book of Daniel relates that an image set up by the king was to be worshipped, when the people heard the sound of six specified instruments. Name three of them.
4. When Miriam and the women of Israel sang of the triumph of their people in the crossing of the Red Sea, they accompanied their song with what instrument?
5. What wind instrument was used in both Old and New Testament times in festal processions, as well as on occasions of both rejoicing and sorrow?

No. 11. BIBLE INCIDENTS

Imagine some one who had attended church and Sunday School up to high school age but never read the Bible through. Sitting down some day to read it, from the beginning as he would any other book, he would often find himself thinking, " Why! I never knew *that* was in the Bible."

How about the following incidents? Can you identify them?
1. The Bible tells us of just one time when Jesus wrote—in the sand, with his finger. It tells us too of one time when he read aloud. Where was it?

[Answers on page 140]

2. One of the apostles once used profane language, and this after he had been with Jesus for a long time. Which one was he?

3. The New Testament describes a foot race between two of the apostles. Who were they? And which was the winner?

4. The Old Testament too tells of a foot race, the man who started with a handicap being the winner. What important news did they carry from the battle front?

5. What apostle escaped from what city in a basket?

No. 12. BIBLE MYTHOLOGY

Six names familiar to readers of Roman mythology are mentioned in the book of Acts, in connection with Paul's journeys. These are: 1. Jupiter. 2. Mercury. 3. Diana. 4. Mars. 5 and 6. Castor and Pollux. Can you tell in what connection each is named?

No. 13. THE BIBLE AND ART

Were you in Europe, studying the history of art, many of the most celebrated pictures and statues in every cathedral and art gallery you visited would be to you meaningless unless you had brought with you some knowledge of the Bible. For instance (and the list might be indefinitely extended) consider the answers to the following questions.

1. Aside from his *Mona Lisa*, what is the best known work of Leonardo da Vinci?

2. What are the most famous statues carved by Michael Angelo?

3. What are his most famous frescoes?

4. What are Raphael's most famous frescoes?

5. What is the most famous of Raphael's easel pictures?

6. Which of Rubens's pictures is best known?

7. What is said to be the largest painting in the world?

8. What of Rembrandt's biblical themes?

Add to which this fact: that it might be said of many a famous artist that more than half the output of his entire life was religious in subject matter.

[Answers on pages 140–141]

No. 14. SUPPLY THE NOUNS (I)

If you can supply the missing nouns in three-fourths of the following Bible quotations, you have passed the test. If you can supply all of them, you have passed *cum laude*. If, in addition, you can give the book from which the quotation is taken, you have passed *magna cum laude*. (No one is expected to be erudite enough to give book, chapter and verse.) In choosing quotations, easy rather than hard ones have been sought. They follow the American Standard Version.

1. The . . . declare the Glory of God.
2. But seek ye first the kingdom of God and his . . .
3. For the wages of sin is . . .
4. They that sow in . . . shall reap in joy.
5. I am the resurrection and the . . .
6. The fear of the Lord is the beginning of . . .
7. As for man, his days are as . . .
8. A . . . that is set upon a hill cannot be hid.
9. The Son of man is Lord of the . . .
10. And he ran before and climbed up into a . . .

No. 15. SUPPLY THE NOUNS (II)

1. And he said, " I know not. Am I my brother's . . . "
2. Consider the . . . of the field, how they grow.
3. Sufficient unto the day is the . . . thereof.
4. Make straight in the . . . a highway for our God.
5. All we, like . . . , have gone astray.
6. The Lord is my . . .
7. God is . . .
8. Wine is a . . .
9. The just shall live by . . .
10. Remember now thy creator in the days of thy . . .

No. 16. SUPPLY THE VERBS

A rule for writers laid down by Ralph Waldo Emerson was, " make the noun and the verb do the work." Can you supply the verbs in the following Bible quotations?

[Answers on pages 141–142]

1. If any man willeth . . . his will, he shall . . . of the teaching.
2. But . . . ye first his kingdom, and his righteousness; and all these things shall be . . . unto you.
3. Thou shalt . . . the Lord, thy God and him only shalt thou . . .
4. As one whom his mother . . . so will I . . . you.
5. My son, if sinners . . . thee . . . thou not.
6. . . . yourselves, therefore, under the mighty hand of God, that he may . . . you in due time.
7. And we . . . that to them that . . . God all things . . . together for good.
8. But if any of you . . . wisdom, let him . . . of God, who . . . to all liberally and upbraideth not.
9. Whether therefore ye . . . , or . . . , or whatsoever ye . . . , do all to the glory of God.
10. He that . . . his transgressions shall not prosper: but whoso . . . and . . . them shall obtain mercy.
11. And he spake a parable unto them, to the end that they ought always to . . . and not to . . .
12. . . . the devil and he will . . . from you.

No. 17. SUPPLY THE ADJECTIVES

Can you supply the adjectives omitted from the following Bible quotations—American Standard Version?
1. Love suffereth long and is . . .
2. He that is . . . in a very little is . . . also in much.
3. He (God) hath made everything . . . in his time.
4. And when the centurion saw what was done, he glorified God, saying, "Certainly this was a . . . man."
5. Thou shalt rise up before the hoary head, and honor the face of the . . . man.
6. Be not . . . in thine own eyes.
7. But . . . and . . . questionings avoid, knowing that they gender strifes.
8. Seest thou a man . . . in his business? He shall stand before kings.

[Answers on pages 142–143]

9. He also that is . . . in his work is brother to him that is a destroyer.
10. And let us not be . . . in well doing.
11. For he grew up before him as a . . . plant: and as a root out of a . . . ground.
12. A . . . heart is a good medicine.

No. 18. BIBLE "BECAUSES"

The most common words are often the most significant, as witness the following. Fill in, if you can, the words omitted from the following Bible quotations (all from the King James Version).

1. We know that we have passed from death unto life, because . . .
2. Because . . . which leadeth unto life and few there be that find it.
3. The hireling fleeth because . . .
4. But if Christ be in you, the body is dead because . . . but the spirit is life because . . .
5. Neither shalt thou swear by thy head, because . . .
6. We love him because . . .
7. Because . . . ye shall live also.

No. 19. BIBLE "WHYS"

"Why" is so common a word that the ordinary concordance makes no attempt to give all the places in which it is found in our Bibles. Nevertheless it is often highly significant. Can you supply the words which follow it in the following quotations? (References are from the King James Version.)

1. And the house was filled with the odor of the ointment. Then said one of his disciples, Judas Iscariot, Simon's son, which should betray him, "Why . . ."
2. And why . . . perceivest not the beam that is in thine own eye?
3. And about the eleventh hour he went out and found others standing idle, and saith unto them, "Why . . ." And they said unto him, "Because no man hath hired us."

[Answers on page 143]

4. And he fell to the earth and heard a voice saying unto him, " Saul, Saul, why . . ."
5. And why . . . and do not the things which I say?
6. And the governor answered and said unto them, " Why . . ." But they cried out the more, saying, " Let him be crucified."
7. Behold two men stood by them in shining garments; and as they were afraid and bowed down their faces to the earth, they said unto them, " Why . . ."

No. 20. BIBLE PHRASES

Few people, unless they have made a special study of it, realize how the Bible, " the most popular book in the English language," as it has been called, is woven into the warp and woof of our everyday speech. We constantly quote the Bible, without the least idea that we are doing so. If any one doubts this, let him consider the following twelve phrases: it would be easy to cite twice as many. We all know them but many will be surprised to learn that their source is the Bible. Ask in what book of the Bible they are found and the person who makes a grade of fifty is doing well.
1. A good, old age.
2. The apple of his eye.
3. The valley of decision.
4. The wings of the morning.
5. No discharge in that war.
6. A drop of a bucket.
7. The salt of the earth.
8. The signs of the times.
9. The powers that be.
10. Decently and in order.
11. From strength to strength.
12. Labor of love.

No. 21. BIBLE SIMILES

A well-known hymn describes the Bible as a garden, an armory, a " deep, deep mine," and all rightly enough, because

[Answers on pages 143–144]

for centuries it has been providing writers, thinkers and speakers with flowers, jewels and weapons. The most familiar line of a famous poem of the nineteenth century, Kipling's *Recessional,* is but an echo from the fourth chapter of Deuteronomy, " Lest we forget." The popular play, *Green Pastures,* and a book on a recent list of best sellers, *Lambs in His Bosom,* both take their titles from the Bible and, if one were to go back a generation, he could easily add fifty more titles: *The Valley of Decision, A Certain Rich Man, Prisoners of Hope,* and many others.

Every day we hear Bible quotations without recognizing them as such: " parting of the ways," " at their wits' end," " a drop in the bucket," " the burden and heat of the day," " wars and rumors of wars," " the strife of tongues." Bible figures of speech are among the most vivid and graphic in the language: clearer than noon day—unstable as water—the people arose as one man —the wings of the morning—the dew of their youth. How many of the following can you complete?

1. As the hart panteth after the water brooks . . .
2. Like as a father pitieth his children . . .
3. I have seen the wicked in great power and spreading himself like . . .
4. For yourselves know perfectly that the day of the Lord so cometh as . . .
5. As for man, his days are as . . . as . . .
6. As the crackling of thorns under a pot, so is . . .
7. Look not thou upon the wine when it is red; at the last it . . .
8. As far as the east is from the west . . .
9. A word fitly spoken is like . . .
10. The path of the righteous is as . . .
11. Who is she that looketh forth as the morning, fair as the . . . clear as the . . . terrible as . . .
12. But man is born unto trouble, as . . .
13. In them hath he set a tabernacle for the sun—and rejoiceth as . . .
14. As a ring of gold in a swine's snout so is . . .
15. But let him ask in faith, nothing doubting; for he that doubteth is like . . .

[Answers on pages 144–145]

No. 22. BIBLE METAPHORS

"A metaphor," to pick an impressive definition from one of the textbooks, "is an implied or elliptical comparison of two things in different categories." More simply, it is a compressed simile. When one says, "The Lord is *like* a shepherd," he makes use of a simile. But when the Psalmist sings, "The Lord *is* my shepherd," he utters a metaphor. Any one familiar with the Bible knows that it is filled with such figures of speech, beautiful, forceful and vivid. How many of the following, taken from the American Standard Version, can you identify?

1. Jesus said unto them, "I am the . . . of life; he that cometh to me shall not hunger."
2. I am the . . . ; by me if any man enter in, he shall be saved.
3. I am the true . . . and my Father is the . . .
4. I am the . . . : the . . . layeth down his life for the sheep.
5. I am the . . . and the . . . , the beginning and the end.
6. I am a . . . of Sharon; a . . . of the valleys.
7. Ye are the . . . of the earth.
8. Ye are the . . . of the world.
9. Thy word is a . . . unto my feet and . . . unto my path.
10. The voice of one saying, "Cry." And one said, "What shall I cry?" "All flesh is . . ."
11. I will say of the Lord, he is my . . . and my . . . ; my God, in whom I trust.
12. He will cover thee with his pinions and under his wings shalt thou take refuge; his truth is a . . . and a . . .

No. 23. BIBLE ANTONYMS

Not until one begins looking for them, does he realize how frequent in the Bible is the use of antonyms, that is, words which are directly opposite in meaning, as joy is the antonym of sorrow. See how many of the following you can fill in. (Quotations are from the American Standard Version.)

1. I came not to call the . . . but . . .
2. And God saw everything that he had made and, behold,

[Answers on page 145]

it was very good. And there was . . . and there was . . . , the sixth day.

3. No man can serve two masters: ye cannot serve . . . and . . .

4. The . . . man doeth good to his own soul; but he that is . . . troubles his own flesh.

5. And this is the judgment—and men loved . . . rather than . . .

6. That ye may be sons of your Father which is in heaven; for he maketh his sun to rise on the . . . and the . . . and sendeth his rain on the . . . and on the . . .

7. I have been . . . and now am . . . , yet have I not seen the righteous forsaken.

8. Now we that are . . . ought to bear the infirmities of the . . .

9. . . . exalteth a nation but . . . is a reproach to any people.

10. And the Lord sent Nathan unto David. And he came unto him and said unto him, " There were two men in one city: the one . . . and the other . . . "

11. For this my son was . . . and is . . . again; he was . . . and is . . .

12. And he hath said unto me, my grace is sufficient for thee, for my . . . is made perfect in . . .

No. 24. BIBLE ANTHROPOMORPHISMS

An anthropomorphism (the word sounds rather alarming) is the representation of diety under human form or with human attributes. God, we are told on the highest authority, is a spirit and a spirit has not flesh and bones. Nevertheless human attributes have always been ascribed to God and doubtless always will be, since they serve to bring him nearer to us.

In the following quotations, can you supply the missing (anthropomorphic) words?

1. The eternal God is our refuge and underneath are . . .

2. Behold the Lord's . . . is not shortened that he cannot save; neither his . . . heavy that he cannot hear.

132 [Answers on page 145]

3. . . . of the Lord are in every place, beholding the evil and the good.
4. Who hath measured the waters in . . . and meted out heaven with a span?
5. He that . . . in the heavens will . . . The Lord will have them in derision.

No. 25. ASSORTED QUOTATIONS (I)

Five of the following quotations are from Shakespeare, five from the Bible. Can you tell which are biblical, which Shakespearean?
1. A man more sinned against than sinning.
2. Is thy servant a dog that he should do this thing?
3. Mercy . . . an attribute of God himself.
4. Peace, peace! When there is no peace.
5. It is not nor it cannot come to good.
6. Hast thou found me, O mine enemy?
7. Are you good men and true?
8. As easy as lying.
9. A thorn in the flesh.
10. The flowers appear on the earth.

No. 26. ASSORTED QUOTATIONS (II)

Five of the following quotations are from the Bible. Five are from other (classic) sources. You "pass" the test if you tell which are which. If you name the author of each secular quotation, you pass *cum laude*; if you also give the book from which each Bible quotation is taken, you pass *magna cum laude*.
1. God tempers the wind to the shorn lamb.
2. Prove all things, hold fast that which is good.
3. God is his own interpreter.
4. Deep calleth unto deep.
5. Hell is paved with good intentions.
6. My days are swifter than a weaver's shuttle.
7. Bread is the staff of life.
8. I have been a stranger in a strange land.
9. The world, the flesh and the devil.

[Answers on pages 145–146]

10. Let me die the death of the righteous and let my last end be like his.

No. 27. PROVERBS: BIBLE AND SECULAR

Five of the following quotations are from the Book of Proverbs. Five are from secular literature. (The ultimate source of all but one of the latter is doubtful.) Can you tell which are which?
1. It hurteth not the tongue to give fair words.
2. A wise son maketh a glad father.
3. God never sends the mouth but he sendeth meat.
4. A merry heart doeth good, like a medicine.
5. Blessings brighten as they take their flight.
6. The liberal soul shall be made fat.
7. It is hard for an empty bag to stand upright.
8. Riches certainly make themselves wings.
9. Man proposes, God disposes.
10. In the multitude of counsellors there is safety.

No. 28. BIBLE OR HYMNAL?

In church, in Sunday School and in Christian homes, one hears every day bits of familiar quotations which are hastily credited to the Bible but which have other sources—though worthy ones. Thus "whose service is perfect freedom" comes from the Book of Common Prayer and the Slough of Despond and the Delectable Mountains are not mentioned in the Bible but in *The Pilgrim's Progress*. Of the following, five are from the Bible and five from familiar hymns. Can you tell which are which? Also, can you name the hymn or the book of the Bible from which each is taken? Where a quotation is simply carried over, word for word, into a hymn, it should of course be credited to the Bible.
1. From strength to strength.
2. From shore to shore.
3. A land of pure delight.
4. Conquering and to conquer.
5. A weary land.

[Answers on page 146]

6. Clearer than noonday.
7. Crown my journey's end.
8. Life's varying scene.
9. The strife of tongues.
10. What time the tempest rages.

No. 29. BIBLE ROOTS OF THE SPIRITUALS

Some of us were brought up on the Spirituals and have heard them sung by Negro "mammies," field hands, roustabouts on the river steamers. Others have heard them on concert platforms from the lips of great artists, for their value as folk music has now come to be universally recognized. For years no one dreamed of reducing them to writing, and yet their origin is fundamentally much like that of the hymns of our own race. They voice the same religious emotions; they contain fervent prayers and exhortations that rise at times almost to ecstasy. Again, like our own hymns, there is hardly one that is not rooted in some story or phrase of the Scriptures.

In the case of the following, most of them quite well known, can you cite the Bible incident to which the song owes its inspiration?

1. I Am Climbing Jacob's Ladder.
2. Go Down, Moses.
3. Stand Still, Jordan.
4. Joshua Fit the Battle of Jericho.
5. Little David Play on Yo' Harp.
6. Swing Low, Sweet Chariot.
7. 'Ziekel Saw the Wheel.
8. Didn't My Lord Deliver Daniel?
9. Ride on King Jesus.
10. Somebody's Knocking at Your Door.

No. 30. BIBLE CHOICES

This is hardly a test of memory, since absolutely correct answers to the following questions would demand a plebescite of Christendom. (Unless, indeed, one were to permit the use of what is said to be the correct answer to all questions, "That

[Answers on pages 146–147]

depends.") The answers you will give call for taste and judgment.

1. What is the most familiar chapter in the whole Bible?
2. What chapter is, from a literary point of view, the most beautiful?
3. What book of the Bible has, in proportion to its length, furnished the greatest number of well-known quotations?
4. Omitting Mary, the mother of Jesus, what woman of the Bible is most widely known?
5. What are the three best known Psalms?
6. Counting *Samuel, Kings* and *Chronicles* each as one book, instead of two, which is your favorite historical book?
7. Who is your favorite Old Testament character?
8. Who is your favorite prophet?
9. What is the best known verse in the Old Testament?
10. What is the best short story in the Old Testament?
11. What is the best short story in the New Testament?
12. Which is the best loved of the four gospels?

ANSWERS

Section VIII
MISCELLANEOUS QUIZZES

No. 1. WHAT THE BIBLE SAYS ABOUT MONEY

1. " How hardly shall they that have riches enter into the kingdom of God " (Mark 10: 23).
2. The parable of the Talents (Matt. 25: 14–30).
3. " Give not that which is holy unto dogs, neither cast your pearls before swine " (Matt. 7: 6).
4. He was not " rich toward God " (Luke 12: 21).
5. The anointing at Bethany (John 12: 1–8).
6. That it should be unostentatious, " in secret," the right hand not knowing what the left hand did (Matt. 6: 1–4).
7. The parable of the Laborers in the Vineyard (Matt. 20: 1–16).
8. " Upon the first day of the week, let each one of you lay by him in store, as he may prosper " (I Cor. 16: 2).
9. " . . . not grudgingly, or of necessity, for God loveth a cheerful (hilarious) giver " (II Cor. 9: 7).
10. That it is a " root of all evil " (I Tim. 6: 10).

No. 2. WHAT THE BIBLE SAYS ABOUT WISDOM

1. The fear of the Lord is the beginning of wisdom (Psalm 111: 10).
2. Wisdom crieth without, she uttereth her voice in the street (Prov. 1: 20–21).
3. Man knoweth not the price thereof . . . it cannot be gotten for gold (Job 28: 13–15).
4. . . . whoso findeth me (wisdom) findeth life and shall obtain favor of the Lord (Prov. 8: 35).

5. By me (wisdom) kings reign and princes decree justice (Prov. 8: 15).

6. A man's wisdom maketh his face to shine and the boldness (Amer. Rev. "hardness") of his face shall be changed (Eccl. 8: 1).

7. Then I saw that wisdom excelleth folly as far as light excelleth darkness (Eccl. 2: 13).

8. For wisdom is a defence and money is a defence but . . . (Eccl. 7: 12).

9. Wisdom is better than weapons of war (Eccl. 9: 18).

10. I (wisdom) love them that love me and they that seek me early shall find me (Prov. 8: 17).

No. 3. WHAT THE BIBLE TELLS US ABOUT LOVE

1. I Cor. 13.

2. Opinions may differ. My own vote would be for the first three words of verse 8: "Love never faileth."

3. "Love worketh no ill to his neighbor; love therefore is the fulfilling of the law" (Rom. 13: 10).

4. "There is no fear in love but perfect love casteth out fear" (I John 4: 18).

5. Yes. (See Deut. 6: 5.) Other references might be given.

6. "Thou shalt love thy neighbor as thyself" (Lev. 19: 18). Jesus was quoting law to a lawyer, when he gave his first and second commandments.

7. John says no. (See I John 4: 20.)

8. "We love him because he first loved us" (I John 4: 19).

9. "That ye may be the children of your Father which is in heaven, for he maketh the sun to rise on the evil and the good and sending rain on the just and the unjust" (Matt. 5: 45). (St. Francis calls this "the great *courtesy* of God.")

10. "This is my commandment, that ye love one another *as I have loved you*" (John 15: 12).

No. 4. BIBLE OCCUPATIONS

1. A herdsman (Gen. 4: 20).

2. A musician and maker of musical instruments (Gen. 4: 21).

3. A worker in metals (Gen. 4: 22).
4. A hunter (Gen. 10: 8–9).
5. A herdsman " and a dresser of sycamore trees " (Amos 7: 14).
6. Fishermen (Matt. 4: 18).
7. A beggar (Luke 16: 20).
8. A taxgatherer (Luke 19: 2).
9. A silversmith (Acts 19: 24).
10. A tanner (Acts 9: 43).
11. A professional solder, holding the rank of centurion (Acts 10: 1).
12. A tent maker (Acts 18: 3).
13. A coppersmith (II Tim. 4: 14).

No. 5. BIBLE LETTERS

1. Romans, First and Second Corinthians, Galatians, Ephesians, Philippians, Colossians, First and Second Thessalonians.
2. James, First and Second Peter, First, Second and Third John, Jude.
3. First and Second Timothy, Titus, Philemon.
4. Hebrews.
5. It is addressed to " the seven churches which are in Asia " (Rev. 1: 4).

No. 6. BIBLE WILD ANIMALS

1. The lion and the bear (I Sam. 17: 36).
2. The foxes (Matt. 8: 20).
3. The leopard (Jer. 13: 23).
4. The wolf (John 10: 12).

No. 7. BIRDS OF THE BIBLE

1. The ravens (I Kings 17: 6).
2. The dove (Psalm 55: 6).
3. The swallow (Psalm 84: 3).
4. The hen (Matt. 23: 37).

No. 8. BIBLE INSECTS

1. There are four specific references to bees, the most dramatic being that of the swarm in the carcase of the lion slain by Samson (Judges 14: 8) and which he made the theme of his riddle.

2. Leviticus 11: 22 makes it lawful to eat locusts. They are commonly mentioned as a scourge, Joel 2: 25 being a typical reference.

3. Flies were one of the plagues sent upon Pharaoh (Ex. 8: 21).

4. Grasshoppers are several times mentioned as an illustration of vast numbers. The most poetic reference is that of the time when "the grasshopper shall be a burden" (Eccl. 12: 5).

5. Ants are mentioned but twice in the Bible, both times as a worthy example of an industrious and provident "people" (Prov. 6: 6 and 30: 25).

No. 9. BIBLE WEAPONS

1. ... righteousness.
2. ... faith.
3. ... salvation.
4. ... the Spirit, which is the word of God (Eph. 6: 13–17).

No. 10. BIBLE MUSICAL INSTRUMENTS

1. The harp (I Sam. 16: 16).
2. The trumpet (Judges 7).
3. The instruments named are: flute, harp, sackbut, psaltery, cornet, and dulcimer (Daniel 3: 5).
4. The timbrel (Ex. 15: 20).
5. The pipe (I Sam. 10: 5; Jer. 48: 36; Luke 7: 32).

No. 11. BIBLE INCIDENTS

1. In the synagogue of his home town (Luke 4: 16–21).
2. Peter: when accused, after Jesus' arrest, of being one of his followers (Mark 14: 71).
3. Peter and John--John won (John 20: 4).

4. That of the complete collapse of Absalom's rebellion (II Sam. 18: 19–33).

5. Paul from Damascus (Acts 9: 23–25).

No. 12. BIBLE MYTHOLOGY

1. Because of a healing performed at Lystra, the pagan priests sought to offer sacrifice to Barnabas as Jupiter and

2. to Paul as Mercury, " because he was the chief speaker " (Acts 14).

3. Diana is mentioned in connection with her temple, one of " the seven wonders of the world," at Ephesus and the riot raised there by Demetrius the silversmith and others of his craft (Acts 19).

4. It was " in the midst of Mars Hill " that Paul preached his sermon to the Athenians (Acts 17).

5 and 6. This was the " sign " or figurehead of the Alexandrian ship in which Paul sailed from Malta. (The American Version translates it *The Twin Brothers.*) (Acts 28: 11.)

No. 13. THE BIBLE AND ART

1. The Fresco of *The Last Supper,* at Milan.

2. Probably his *Moses* and his *Young David.*

3. Those on the walls of the Sistine Chapel at Rome, their subjects wholly biblical.

4. Those in the Vatican—most of them biblical.

5. Most critics would probably say his *Sistine Madonna* in Dresden, or his *Transfiguration,* in Rome.

6. Probably his *Descent from the Cross,* in Antwerp.

7. The *Paradise,* of Tintoretto, on the walls of the Doges' Palace in Venice.

8. Both the Old and New Testaments might be richly illustrated, using only Rembrandt's etchings.

No. 14. SUPPLY THE NOUNS (I)

1. —heavens . . . (Psalm 19: 1).

2. —righteousness (Matt. 6: 33).

3. —death (Rom. 6: 23).
4. —tears . . . (Psalm 126: 5).
5. —life (John 11: 25).
6. —wisdom (Psalm 111: 10).
7. —grass (Psalm 103: 15).
8. —city . . . (Matt. 5: 14).
9. —Sabbath (Luke 6: 5).
10. —sycamore tree (Luke 19: 4).

No. 15. SUPPLY THE NOUNS (II)

1. —" keeper? " (Gen. 4: 9). (One writer has suggested that he was right: he was not his brother's keeper: but he was his brother's *brother*.)
2. —lilies . . . (Matt. 6: 28).
3. —evil . . . (Matt. 6: 34).
4. —desert . . . (Isaiah 40: 3).
5. —sheep . . . (Isaiah 53: 6).
6. —shepherd (Psalm 23: 1).
7. —love (I John 4: 8).
8. —mocker (Prov. 20: 1).
9. —faith (Hab. 2: 4).
10. —youth (Eccles. 12: 1).

No. 16. SUPPLY THE VERBS

1. —to do . . . know . . . (John 7: 17).
2. —seek . . . added . . . (Matt. 6: 33).
3. —worship . . . serve (Luke 4: 8).
4. —comforteth . . . comfort . . . (Isaiah 66: 13).
5. —entice . . . consent . . . (Prov. 1: 10).
6. Humble . . . exalt . . . (I Peter 5: 6).
7. —know . . . love . . . work (Rom. 8: 28).
8. —lack . . . ask . . . giveth . . . (Jas. 1: 5).
9. —eat . . . drink . . . do . . . (I Cor. 10: 31).
10. —covereth . . . confesseth . . . forsaketh . . . (Prov. 28: 13).
11. —pray . . . faint (Luke 18: 1).
12. Resist . . . flee . . . (Jas. 4: 7).

No. 17. SUPPLY THE ADJECTIVES

1. —kind (I Cor. 13: 4).
2. —faithful—faithful (Luke 16: 10).
3. —beautiful . . . (Eccl. 3: 11).
4. —righteous (Luke 23: 47).
5. —old . . . (Lev. 19: 32).
6. —wise . . . (Prov. 3: 7).
7. —foolish . . . ignorant . . . (II Tim. 2: 23).
8. —diligent . . . (Prov. 22: 29).
9. —slack . . . (Prov. 18: 9).
10. —weary . . . (Gal. 6: 9).
11. —tender . . . dry . . . (Isaiah 53: 2).
12. —cheerful . . . (Proverbs 17: 22).

No. 18. BIBLE "BECAUSES"

1. —we love the brethren (I John 3: 14).
2. —straight is the gate and narrow is the way . . . (Matt. 7: 14).
3. —he is an hireling and careth not for the sheep (John 10: 13).
4. —of sin . . . of righteousness (Rom. 8: 10).
5. —thou canst not make one hair white or black (Matt. 5: 36).
6. —he first loved us (I John 4: 19).
7. —I live . . . (John 14: 19).

No. 19. BIBLE "WHYS"

1. ". . . was not the ointment sold for three hundred pence and given to the poor?" (John 12: 3–5).
2. ". . . beholdest thou the mote that is in thy brother's eye and . . . (Luke 6: 41).
3. ". . . stand ye here all the day idle?" (Matt. 20: 6–7).
4. ". . . persecutest thou me?" (Acts 9: 4).
5. ". . . call ye me Lord, Lord . . ." (Luke 6: 46).
6. ". . . what evil hath he done?" (Matt. 27: 23).
7. ". . . seek ye the living among the dead?" (Luke 24: 4–6).

No. 20. BIBLE PHRASES

1. Gen. 15: 15.
2. Deut. 32: 10.
3. Joel 3: 14.
4. Psalm 139: 9.
5. Eccl. 8: 8.
6. Isa. 40: 15.
7. Matt. 5: 13.
8. Matt. 16: 3.
9. Rom. 13: 1.
10. I Cor. 14: 40.
11. Psalm 84: 7.
12. I Thess. 1: 3.

No. 21. BIBLE SIMILES

1. . . . so panteth my soul after thee, O God (Psalm 42: 1).
2. . . . so the Lord pitieth them that fear him (Psalm 103: 13).
3. . . . a green bay tree (Psalm 37: 35).
4. . . . a thief in the night (I Thess. 5: 2).
5. . . . grass; . . . a flower of the field, so he flourisheth (Psalm 103: 15).
6. . . . the laughter of the fool (Eccl. 7: 6).
7. . . . biteth like a serpent and stingeth like an adder (Prov. 23: 31–32).
8. . . . so far hath he removed our transgressions from us (Psalm 103: 12).
9. . . . apples of gold in network of silver (Prov. 25: 11).
10. . . . the dawning light that shineth more and more until the perfect day (Prov. 4: 18).
11. . . . moon, . . . sun, . . . an army with banners (Song of Solomon 6: 10).
12. . . . the sparks fly upward (Job 5: 7).
13. . . . a strong man to run his course (Psalm 19: 4–5).
14. . . . a fair woman that is without discretion (Prov. 11: 22).

15. . . . the surge of the sea, driven by the wind and tossed (Jas. 1: 6).

No. 22. BIBLE METAPHORS

1. Bread (John 6: 35).
2. Door (John 10: 9).
3. Vine, husbandman (John 15: 1).
4. Good shepherd; good shepherd (John 10: 11).
5. Alpha, Omega (Rev. 22: 13).
6. Rose, lily (Song of Sol. 2: 1).
7. Salt (Matt. 5: 13).
8. Light (Matt. 5: 14).
9. Lamp, light (Psalm 119: 105).
10. Grass (Isaiah 40: 6).
11. Refuge, fortress (Psalm 91: 2).
12. Shield, buckler (Psalm 91: 4).

No. 23. BIBLE ANTONYMS

1. Righteous, sinners (Matt. 9: 13).
2. Evening, morning (Gen. 1: 31).
3. God, mammon (Matt. 6:24).
4. Merciful, cruel (Prov. 11: 17).
5. Darkness, light (John 3: 19).
6. Evil, good. Just, unjust (Matt. 5: 45).
7. Young, old (Psalm 37: 25).
8. Strong, weak (Rom. 15: 1).
9. Righteousness, sin (Prov. 14: 34).
10. Rich, poor (II Sam. 12: 1).
11. Dead, alive. Lost, found (Luke 15: 24).
12. Power, weakness (II Cor. 12: 9).

No. 24. BIBLE ANTHROPOMORPHISMS

1. . . . the everlasting arms (Deut. 33: 27).
2. . . . hand . . . ear . . . (Isaiah 59: 1).
3. The eyes . . . (Prov. 15: 3).
4. . . . hollow of his hand . . . (Isaiah 40: 12).
5. . . . sitteth . . . laugh . . . (Psalm 2: 4).

No. 25. ASSORTED QUOTATIONS (I)

1. Shakespeare, *King Lear.*
2. II Kings 8: 13.
3. Shakespeare, *Merchant of Venice.*
4. Jeremiah 6: 14.
5. Shakespeare, *Hamlet.*
6. I Kings 21: 20.
7. Shakespeare, *Much Ado About Nothing.*
8. Shakespeare, *Hamlet.*
9. II Cor. 12: 7.
10. Song of Solomon 2: 12.

No. 26. ASSORTED QUOTATIONS (II)

1. Laurence Sterne.
2. I Thess. 5: 21.
3. William Cowper.
4. Psalm 42: 7.
5. Samuel Johnson.
6. Job 7: 6.
7. Jonathan Swift.
8. Exodus 2: 22.
9. Book of Common Prayer.
10. Numbers 23: 10.

No. 27. PROVERBS: BIBLE AND SECULAR

Numbers 1, 3, 5, 7 and 9 are secular.
Numbers 2, 4, 6, 8 and 10 are biblical.

No. 28. BIBLE OR HYMNAL?

1. Psalm 84: 7.
2. Jesus Shall Reign Where'er the Sun.
3. There is a Land of Pure Delight.
4. Revelation 6: 2.
5. Isaiah 32: 2.
6. Job 11: 17.

7. Father, Whate'er of Earthly Bliss.
8. O Holy Savior, Friend Unseen.
9. Psalm 31: 20.
10. O God, the Rock of Ages.

No. 29. BIBLE ROOTS OF THE SPIRITUALS

1. Gen. 28.
2. Ex. 3: 10.
3. Joshua 3.
4. Joshua 6.
5. I Sam. 16: 23.
6. II Kings 2: 11.
7. Ezek. 1: 16.
8. Dan. 6: 22.
9. John 12: 12–15.
10. Rev. 3: 20.

No. 30. BIBLE CHOICES

1. Since the Sermon on the Mount consists of several chapters, a pretty good case can be made out for the 23rd Psalm or for I Corinthians 13.
2. In his *Literary Taste*, Arnold Bennett says some interesting things about *Isaiah* chapter forty.
3. Probably *Ecclesiastes*.
4. Probably Eve.
5. The 23rd Psalm will of course be named for first place, with (probably) a wide variety among the choices for second and third places. Perhaps the first? Perhaps the hundredth? Perhaps the nineteenth?
6. My own choice would be *Samuel*—a perfect mine of thrilling adventure stories.
7. A world figure: Moses? David? Or some comparatively obscure man: Caleb? Jonathan?
8. Most people would probably say Isaiah.
9. To ask this question about the *New* Testament would be altogether too easy.

10. The choice would probably lie between the stories of Ruth and Joseph.

11. The choice should lie between The Prodigal Son and The Good Samaritan.

12. Ernest Renan, the French scholar, author of *The Life of Jesus,* called the gospel of Luke " the most beautiful book in the world."